Local Government Finance
in Ireland

Maurice Coughlan and Donal de Buitleir

First published 1996
by the Institute of Public Administration,
57-61 Lansdowne Road,
Dublin, Ireland.

British Library Cataloguing in Publication Data

Cover design by Butler Claffey Design

ISBN 1 872002 28 5

Typeset by Computertype Ltd.
Printed by Smurfit Print, Dublin

Contents

ABBREVIATIONS

CSO   Central Statistics Office

EAGGF   European Agricultural Guidance and Guarantee Fund

EMU   Economic and Monetary Union

ERDF   European Regional Development Fund

ESF   European Social Fund

ESRI   Economic and Social Research Institute

EU   European Union

FÁS   An Foras Aiseanna Saothair

GDP   Gross Domestic Product

GNP   Gross National Product

NESC   National Economic and Social Council

OECD   Organisation for Economic Co-operation and Development

PCP   Public Capital Programme

RSG   Rate Support Grant

VAT   Value Added Tax

VEC   Vocational Education Committee

CHRONOLOGY

1972   White Paper on Local Finance and Taxation
        published.

1973-77 Public housing and health service costs taken
        off the rates and transferred to central
        government.

1975   ERDF established.

1977   One quarter of domestic rates met by central
        government.

1978   End of rates on domestic etc. property; domestic
        rate grant introduced along with limits on local
        rating powers.

1982   High Court decided that rates on land were
        unconstitutional; Agricultural Grant subsequently
        became a grant to compensate local authorities
        for the absence of rates on land; a shortfall
        occurred in the level of the domestic rate
        grant.

1983   Central government ceased to exercise control
        over the level of increases in rates on
        commercial/industrial property; rate grants no
        longer to meet in full rates income foregone;
        Local Government (Financial Provisions) (No.2)
        Act widened local charging powers.

1984   *January:* Supreme Court confirmed High Court
        decision on rates on land, in different terms.

1985   NESC and Commission on Taxation reports on local government finance published; Naas UDC removed from office for failure to adopt an estimate of expenses (which included revenue from domestic service charges) – the council was replaced by a commissioner.

1986   Supplementary welfare allowance demand payable by local authorities to health boards ended. This and other later reductions in expenditure demands on local authorities were balanced by downward adjustment of central government grants.

1986   *November:* Farm Tax levied by local authorities.

1987   Local authority payments to the Office of Public Works in respect of arterial drainage ended.

1987   *March:* Farm Tax abolished.

1988   Local authority liability to make certain loan repayments to the Local Loans Fund ended; 100% central government funding introduced for a number of local capital programmes; payments to ACOT ended; RSG formed by amalgamation of domestic and agricultural rate grants and bounty in lieu of rates on government property.

1989   ESB began to pay rates directly to local authorities.

1989-93   First period of EU assistance under reformed Structural Funds.

1991   Report of Advisory Expert Committee on Local Government Reorganisation and Reform published ('the Barrington Report').

1993 EU Cohesion Fund established; fisheries recoupment, to compensate local authorities for rates exemption for private fisheries, merged with RSG; value for money unit established in local government audit service; National Roads Authority and Environmental Protection Agency established.

1994 Regional authorities established; specific grant introduced for improvement works on non-national roads (EU-aided); grant to meet 50 per cent of cost of preparing and maintaining the electoral register merged with RSG.

December: New Government programme, *A Government of Renewal,* indicated that a study of local government finance would be undertaken; domestic service charges to be allowed against income tax commencing in the tax year 1996-97.

1994-99 Second period of EU assistance under reformed Structural Funds.

1995 *July:* Local Government (Delimitation of Water Supply Disconnection Powers) Act, 1995 enacted, setting out procedures to be followed by local authorities when disconnecting consumers for non-payment of domestic water charges. Restoration programme announced for regional and county roads.

November: Securitisation (Proceeds of Certain Mortgages) Act, 1995 enacted to allow part of the local authority housing loan portfolio to be securitised.

PREFACE

The origins of this book lie in a need identified by the Institute of Public Administration for a textbook for its students of local government finance.

We are grateful to the many people in the Institute who assisted us in bringing the project to fruition. We are also grateful for comments on early drafts received from a number of readers. Any errors or omissions remaining are our responsibility.

The book is based on published documents and other public sources which are detailed in notes to the chapters. Where opinions are expressed, they are ours alone and do not imply any views on the part of our employing organisations.

The book reflects the factual position in relation to local government finance as it stood at December 1995.

1
INTRODUCTION

This book is an introduction to the arrangements for financing local government in Ireland, and to theoretical approaches to local finance. While much has been written about local government finance, there is no single up-to-date account of local financial arrangements, or any theoretical treatment of the issue in Ireland other than in the context of specific recommendations for policy change. The aim of this book is to fill this gap.

It is not intended to prescribe a solution to the 'problem' of local government finance, as this would involve a political choice. Rather, the aim is to describe the present system, set out the issues involved and give the interested reader a framework and some analytical tools to evaluate the existing system and any amendments that might be proposed.

Structure of Book
Chapter 2 sets out the background against which the issue of local government finance must be considered. It details the role and functions of local authorities and the various capital investment programmes managed by them. It examines current income and expenditure and places local government finance in a wider international and macroeconomic context.

Chapter 3 deals with the issue of central-local relations. Particular attention is paid to the impact of Ireland's membership of the EU.

Chapter 4 considers the case for local taxation and outlines the criteria which may be used to evaluate a system of local taxation.

Chapter 5 outlines the valuation and rating systems and describes how rates came to be limited to commercial/industrial property.

Chapter 6 looks at options for increasing the share of local taxation in the overall financing of local government, if this is desired as an objective of public policy. Particular attention is paid to the possibilities of local motor tax, property tax, income tax, VAT and environmental taxes.

Chapter 7 examines the role of central government grants in local government finance. It details the main reasons for these grants, analyses the main types of grant and discusses some issues in relation to the present system in Ireland.

Chapter 8 considers the principles which apply in levying charges for local authority services, and looks at the scope for increasing revenue from this source.

Chapter 9 draws conclusions.

Throughout this book the phrases 'local government' or 'local authorities', when used in an Irish context, mean county borough corporations, county councils, borough corporations and urban district councils, as shown in Figure 1. They do not include regional authorities, town commissioners or other miscellaneous bodies which have more limited remits within the local government system, or other sub-national public bodies.

Figure 1: Local Authorities in Ireland

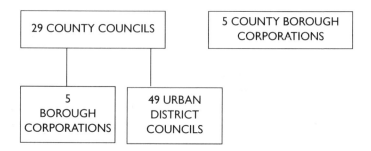

2
BACKGROUND

Introduction

This chapter details the role and functions of Irish local authorities and how these compare with the responsibilities of local authorities in other countries. The various capital investment programmes managed by local authorities are discussed. Details are then given of current expenditure and income and further international comparisons are made. Finally, the issues of local expenditure and taxation are placed in a wider macroeconomic and public finance context.

Role of Local Authorities

In 1995, local authorities were responsible for an estimated £1126 million in current expenditure and for a further £764 million in capital spending.[1] Total expenditure of £1890 million represented 13.6 per cent of total public expenditure in 1995, 4.9 per cent of estimated GDP for that year and 5.6 per cent of GNP.[2] While in absolute terms local authorities use a considerable volume of national resources, by international standards these figures are low.

Systems of local government finance have to be considered in the context of their function in assisting local authorities in the performance of the role assigned to them. Table 1 sets out the principal functions of local authorities. In general, county borough corporations, county councils, borough corporations and urban district councils are the housing, road, sanitary and planning authorities for their areas. They also provide environmental and certain other services to the local community.[3] Traditionally, local authorities have been constrained from moving beyond this largely infrastructural and environmental remit by the doctrine of

Table 1: Principal Functions of Local Authorities★

PROGRAMME GROUPS	FUNCTIONS
Housing and Building	■ Assessment of housing needs ■ Provision, management, maintenance and improvement of social housing ■ Assistance to voluntary housing bodies ■ Shared ownership scheme ■ Assistance to persons housing themselves or improving their houses ■ Accommodation for homeless ■ Travellers' accommodation ■ Enforcement of housing standards
Road Transportation and Safety	■ Road maintenance ■ Road improvement ■ Public lighting ■ Traffic management ■ Road safety ■ Motor taxation ■ Vehicle testing ■ Driver licensing
Water Supply and Sewerage	■ Provision, operation and maintenance of public water supply and sewerage facilities ■ Public conveniences
Development Incentives and Controls	■ Development plans ■ Development control ■ Building control ■ Promotion of development ■ Urban and village renewal ■ Twinning
Environmental Protection	■ Environmental management planning ■ Licensing of emissions/activities ■ Enforcement of environmental controls ■ Environmental improvement and awareness ■ Waste collection and disposal ■ Litter control

Table 1: (contd.)

Environmental Protection (contd.)	■ Burial grounds ■ Dangerous buildings ■ Fire fighting and safety
Recreation and Amenity	■ Swimming pools ■ Libraries ■ Parks and open spaces ■ Recreation centres ■ The arts ■ Derelict sites
Agriculture, Education, Health and Welfare	■ Contribution to vocational education committees ■ Higher education grants
Miscellaneous	■ Elections ■ Courthouses ■ Consumer protection ■ Coroners and inquests ■ Malicious damage to property

Sources: Department of the Environment, *Local Government and the Elected Member 1991* and *Local Authority Estimates 1995.*

* These functions are not necessarily the responsibility of each category of local authority to the same extent.

ultra vires, under which specific legislative sanction was required before a local authority could take any particular action. However, the Local Government Act, 1991 (section 6) relaxed this constraint by giving local authorities a general power to act to promote the interests of the local community.

Irish local authorities, therefore, perform a significant range of functions which impact in varying ways on the lives of the local community, whether through the provision of a house to those in need, the repair of a road damaged by poor weather, the supply of water, the disposal of refuse or a myriad other means. However, in attempting to gauge the importance of local authorities, it is instructive to compare these local government functions with international standards. Table 2 sets out, for fifteen European

Table 2: Functions of European Local Authorities

Functional Classification	Aus	Bel	Den	Fra	Ger	Ire	Ital	Lux	Neth	Nor	Port	Swe	Swit	Turk	UK
Refuse collection and disposal	L	L	L	L	L	L	L	L	L	L	L	L	L,R	L	L
Slaughterhouses	L	L	L	L	L	L	L	L	L	L	L	L	L	L	L
Theatres, concerts	L,R	L		L	L,R		L,R	L	L	L	L	L	L	L	L
Museums, art galleries, libraries	L	L,R	L,R	L,R	L,R	L	L,R	L	L	L	L	L,R	L	L,R	L
Parks and open spaces	L	L,R	L	L,R	L	L	L,R	L	L,R	L	L	L	L	L,R	L
Sports and leisure pursuits	L	L,R	L	L	L,R	L	L,R	L	L,R	L	L	L	L	L	L
Roads	L,R	L,R	L,R	L,R	L,R	L	L,R	L	L,R	L,R	L	L	L,R	L,R	L
Urban road transport	L		L	L,R	L,R		L,R	L	L	L	L	L,R	L	L	L
Ports		L			L,R		L	L	L	L	L	L	R		
Airports					R		L	L	L	L		L,R	R		L
District heating	L	L	L	L	L		L					L	L,R	L	
Water supply	L	L	L	L	L	L	L,R	L	L,R	L	L	L	L	L,R	L(c)
Agriculture, forestry, fishing, hunting	R	L,R		L,R	L,R		L,R		L	L,R	L	L	L,R	L,R	L
Electricity		L,R	L		L		L		L,R	L	L	L	L,R	L	
Commerce	L,R	L		L	L,R		L,R		L,R	L	L	L	L,R	L,R	
Tourism	L,R	L,R		L,R	L,R	L	R		L	L	L	L,R	L,R	L,R	L

Security, police	L	L	L	L,R	L	L	L	L,R	L	L,R	L
Fire protection	L	L	L,R	L	L	L	L	L	L	L,R	L
Justice			R		L,R				L,R		L
Pre-school education	L,R	L	L	L	L	L	L		L	L,R	L
Primary and secondary education	L,R	L,R	L(a)	L,R	L,R	L(b)	L	L,R	L(b)	L,R	L
Vocational and technical training	R	L,R	L	L	L,R	L	L,R		L,R	L,R	L
Higher education		L,R	R	L,R						R	L
Adult education	L	L	L,R	R	L	L,R	L	L,R		L,R	L
Hospitals and convalescent homes	L,R	L,R	L,R	L,R	L	L,R	L,R	R	R	L,R	L,R
Personal health	L,R	L	L,R	L,R	L	L	L	R	R	R	R
Family welfare services	L,R	L,R	L,R	L,R	L	L	L	L,R	L	L,R	L
Welfare homes	LR	L	L	L	L	L	L	L,R	L	L,R	L
Housing	L,R	L	L,R	L,R	L,R	L	L	L	L	L	L
Town planning	L	L	L	L,R	L	L	L	L,R	L	L,R	L

(a) Mainly Primary Education

(b) Primary Education only

(c) Scotland only

L = Local Governments

R = Regional Governments (including state governments; Departments in France; and Provinces in Italy)

Source: Council of Europe, 'Financial Apportionment and Equalisations 1981', reprinted in *Report of Advisory Expert Committee on Local Government Reorganisation and Reform*, 1991, p. 86.

countries (including Ireland), the functions assigned to local government. It highlights what has been described as 'the existing very narrow range of Irish local government services'.[4] 'In any comparison with other European countries it is apparent that Ireland has far fewer functions which are the responsibility of local government (or regional government in those countries which have a regional tier)'.[5]

It is particularly noteworthy that local authorities in Ireland do not have a significant role in some services which are viewed as essential in the modern state: public transport, energy supply, police and security, education, health and social welfare. Furthermore, many initiatives in the local development area in recent years (e.g. County Enterprise Boards, Area Partnership Companies, the LEADER programme, the Western Development Partnership Board, County Strategy Groups) have taken place outside the formal local government system, though not unrelated to it.[6] The conclusion must be that while local authorities are important in Ireland, they are not as important here as they are in some other democracies.

Local Authorities and the Public Capital Programme

Capital expenditure may be regarded as expenditure on the creation of an asset having a life beyond the year in which it is provided. Each year, as part of its budgetary process, central government publishes a PCP which details the overall allocations for a variety of public sector capital services for the year. The Minister for the Environment makes individual allocations from the PCP to local authorities to finance capital programmes for which they are responsible. In the case of national primary and national secondary roads, the allocations are made by the National Roads Authority which was established under the Roads Act, 1993. Given the multi-annual nature of capital expenditure, allocations cover the cost of ongoing work on schemes started in earlier years as well as the cost of new schemes to begin in the current year. The latter are determined having regard to proposals submitted by local authorities; an assessment of the needs of the area; national and in some cases EU priorities; and the total resources available.

Local authority capital expenditure, consisting of PCP allocations made by the Minister or the National Roads Authority, is financed in a variety of ways depending on the nature of the service. Table 3 summarises estimated local authority capital expenditure within the PCP in 1995 and how this expenditure was to be financed. Although the proportion varies from year to year, it shows that 75 per cent of such expenditure was to be met by central government grants in that year, all of which would be channelled through the Department of the Environment and much of which (as discussed in chapter 3) would be recouped by EU Structural and Cohesion Funds. Particular programmes also rely on internal local authority receipts (i.e. capital income, transfers from current account) and on borrowing.

The following are the principal capital services provided by local authorities:

(i) *Social Housing*

This programme mainly comprises the provision of local authority housing, the purchase of existing private houses as additions to the local authority housing stock, the carrying out of remedial and improvement works to local authority housing, the provision of group housing and halting sites for travellers, and assistance by local authorities to the voluntary housing sector. It is financed, in the case of local authority housing, private house purchases, remedial/improvement works and travellers' accommodation, by a combination of capital grants from central government and internal receipts from the sale of local authority houses under tenant purchase schemes. Local authority capital expenditure on assistance to the voluntary sector is funded by central government grant (in the case of the Capital Assistance Scheme which is focused on special housing needs such as the elderly, homeless or disabled) and by borrowing from the Housing Finance Agency (in the case of the Rental Subsidy Scheme which concentrates on accommodation to meet the needs of low-income families).

Table 3: Local Authority Capital Expenditure and Finance 1995 (Estimated)

Programme	Expenditure (£m)	Finance (£m)		
		Central Government Grants	Internal Receipts	Borrowing
Social Housing				
(i) Local Authority	191	144	47	–
(ii) Voluntary –				
Capital Assistance	15	15	–	–
(iii) Voluntary –				
Rental Subsidy	23	–	–	23
House Purchase and Improvement Loans	99.5	–	48	51.5
Roads				
(i) National	191	191	–	–
(ii) Non-National★	97.5	97.5	–	–
(iii) DTI Traffic Management★	3.5	3.5	–	–
Water and Sewerage Services★	103	103	–	–
Environmental Services	21.5	–	–	21.5
Urban and Village Renewal	8	6	–	2
Fire and Emergency Services	4.5	4.5	–	–
Libraries	3	3	–	–
Swimming Pools★	2	2	–	–
Waste Recovery★	1	1	–	–
Access for Disabled★	0.5	0.5	–	–
TOTAL	**764**	**571**	**95**	**98**

Sources: Department of Finance, *Revised Estimates for Public Services 1995* and *Public Capital Programme 1995.*

★ Excluding limited local authority contributions from internal receipts or borrowing.

(ii) House Purchase and Improvement Loans

This consists for the most part of the shared ownership scheme under which local authorities purchase houses chosen by qualifying applicants. The applicant then buys part (at least 40 per cent) of the equity in the house by way of a mortgage, with the balance being retained by, and rented from, the authority; the applicant is obliged to purchase the remainder of the equity at a later date. This scheme, which is an important element of the social housing programme, has recently been extended to tenant purchasers of local authority houses. Local authority expenditure is funded by borrowing from the Housing Finance Agency.

Local authorities also make funds available for the purchase and improvement of houses to persons who are otherwise unable to obtain loan finance. Local authority activity in providing loans for house purchase has been in decline in recent years, largely reflecting the increased role of building societies and banks as providers of mortgage finance for lower income households. Local authority expenditure is funded by internal receipts from the redemption of mortgages and by borrowing from the Housing Finance Agency.

A recent development in this area, although not one directly affecting local government finance, is the securitisation of loans being repaid by home owners, through local authorities, to the Local Loans Fund which is operated by the Office of Public Works. Under the Securitisation (Proceeds of Certain Mortgages) Act, 1995, part of the stream of local authority income, from housing loans they have made with finance borrowed from the Exchequer through the Local Loans Fund (which provided loan finance in the past), is being paid by the authorities to a company. In return for this assignment the company paid the Exchequer a lump sum at the beginning of the transaction which it raised by issuing bonds. In this way the Exchequer received money up front which, without a securitisation scheme, would have come to it in bi-annual payments from local authorities over a period of years. Payments made to the securitising company by the local authorities are treated, as far as their debt to the Local Loans Fund is concerned, as if they were payments to the Fund. There is no adverse effect on the finances of local authorities and no change in the legal position of the local authorities' mortgagors, who continue to make repayments to local authorities.

(iii) Roads

Roads comprise the second largest element of local authority capital expenditure after housing. As far as the national primary and secondary roads are concerned (i.e. the routes of greatest economic importance due to the volumes of commercial traffic they carry), the National Roads Authority has overall responsibility for improvement works on such roads. Local authorities act as agents for the Authority in the planning and execution of works on these roads. The cost of works is met in full by the Authority which in turn is funded by central government grant; the Authority also has power to pursue toll-based financing options in respect of national roads.

As regards non-national roads (i.e. regional, county and urban roads), central government provides grants to local authorities to finance capital expenditure on these roads and the amount involved has increased substantially in the past decade. Central government assistance is partly in the form of grants which local authorities can use at their discretion, subject to conditions set by the Department. In addition, grants are available to meet the full cost of improvement of specific stretches of non-national roads which will have a significant economic impact, and further Exchequer grants are provided under a restoration programme for regional and county roads in county council areas which was announced in 1995[7]. Some provision is also made under this heading for expenditure on non-national road improvement from local authority own resources (i.e. commercial/industrial rates, RSG etc.).

Local authorities in the area covered by the Dublin Transportation Initiative also receive grants to implement traffic management measures; they must contribute a percentage (varying from 10 to 25 per cent) of the cost involved.

(iv) Water and Sewerage Services

Local authorities are sanitary authorities, responsible for the provision of water supply and sewerage facilities in their areas. With increasing demands for improved drinking water quality and for the elimination of untreated sewage discharges, the cost of this programme has risen sharply in recent years. Central government generally meets the full cost of capital works approved by the Department of the Environment.[8] Grants are provided to meet 75 per cent of the cost of small water and sewerage schemes, and the maximum grant available is £75,000. This sub-programme makes up a small proportion of the overall water and sewerage services capital programme: £2 million in central government grants and £1 million in local authority contributions were devoted to it in 1995[9].

(v) Environmental Services

This programme comprises miscellaneous local authority services such as the construction of local authority offices and the provision of waste disposal facilities; it is financed by borrowing from financial institutions and from the Local Loans Fund.

(vi) Other Services

Local authorities are responsible for a range of smaller-scale capital services including:

- the carrying out of urban and village renewal works – local finance must match central government grants for such works (generally on a 50:50 basis, but 75 Exchequer: 25 local in the case of village renewal);
- fire and emergency services – met in full by central government grants;
- development and improvement of libraries – also met in full by central government grants;
- provision and renovation of swimming pools – central government meets 80 per cent of the cost of new

swimming pools, with the balance being met by local contribution, and meets the full cost of renovation works;

- the provision of waste recovery facilities; generally 50 per cent of the cost is met by central government.

Central government grants for libraries and swimming pools (and for the provision of communal facilities in voluntary housing schemes) are financed by proceeds from the National Lottery.

Current Expenditure

Current expenditure is of a recurring nature and does not result in the acquisition of a permanent asset. Details of estimated local authority current (or revenue) account expenditure in 1995 are given in Table 4. It shows that, as with the capital account, the bulk of expenditure arises on the Housing and Building (21 per cent) and Road Transportation and Safety (21 per cent) Programme Groups. On the housing side, most expenditure is on repayments by local authorities to the Housing Finance Agency or the Local Loans Fund, following earlier borrowing by them to finance loans to individuals for house purchase and improvement, and on management and maintenance of local authority housing. As regards roads, the major item is management and maintenance of national and non-national roads.

The next largest programme group is Environmental Protection (15 per cent), with most expenditure here being devoted to fire protection and waste disposal. Water Supply and Sewerage (12.5 per cent) concerns the operation and maintenance of the often complex and costly pipe networks and treatment facilities associated with these services. Recreation and Amenity (12 per cent) covers the operation of parks, open spaces, recreation centres, libraries and swimming pools. Agriculture, Education, Health and Welfare (9.5 per cent), despite its title, relates for the most part to payment of higher education grants to third-level students.

Miscellaneous Services (6 per cent) deals with financial management, rate collection and a wide variety of other services. Finally, Development Incentives and Controls (3 per cent), while

not important in expenditure terms, relates to the local authority's functions as planning authority, promoting and controlling
development in its area.

Local authorities employ 30,000 people, down from 36,000 in
1983. Wages, salaries, pensions and other personnel costs comprise
about 50 per cent of local authority current expenditure. Such
costs are apportioned amongst the various programmes as
appropriate so that, for example, wages of road workers would be
included in programme 2.1 – Road Upkeep. Salaries which
cannot be attributed to particular programmes (e.g. that of the
County Manager) are apportioned amongst the Administration
and Miscellaneous programme in each programme group.

Current Income

Local authorities have three main sources of current income:
rates, grants from central government and miscellaneous receipts.

Rates are a local tax levied on land, buildings and other
miscellaneous property. Domestic property has been exempt from
rates since 1978 and agricultural land has been treated likewise
since 1982. Today, therefore, rates remain only on commercial/
industrial property and yielded an estimated £323 million in
1995[10]. Valuation and rating are discussed further in chapter 5.

The principal central government grants on current account
are:

- the Rate Support Grant paid by the Department of the Environment to local authorities to compensate them for the
  rate reliefs outlined above, for the absence of rates on
  government property and private fisheries, and for half the
  cost of compiling and maintaining the register of electors
  (1995 – £189 million);
- a grant paid by the Department of Education to meet the
  cost of higher education grants (1995 – £60 million);
- a grant paid by FÁS in respect of Community Employment
  under which part-time training and employment opportunit-
  ies are given to the long-term unemployed (1995 – £44
  million);

Table 4: Local Authority Current Expenditure 1995 (Estimated)

Programme Group and Programmes		Expenditure
1.	**Housing and Building**	**£m**
1.1	Local Authority Housing	73.6
1.2	Assistance to Persons Housing Themselves	111.1
1.3	Assistance to Persons Improving Houses	6.2
1.8	Administration and Miscellaneous	42.4
Less:	Inter-Authority Contributions	0.6
TOTAL		**232.7**
2.	**Road Transportation and Safety**	**£m**
2.1	Road Upkeep	139.8
2.3	Road Traffic	15.0
2.8	Administration and Miscellaneous	81.0
Less:	Inter-Authority Contributions	1.6
TOTAL		**234.2**
3.	**Water Supply and Sewerage**	**£m**
3.1	Public Water Supply Schemes	88.1
3.2	Public Sewerage Schemes	37.4
3.3	Private Installations	0.5
3.8	Administration and Miscellaneous	26.2
Less:	Inter-Authority Contributions	10.2
TOTAL		**142.0**
4.	**Development Incentives and Controls**	**£m**
4.1	Land Use Planning	16.7
4.2	Industrial Development	1.8
4.3	Other Development and Promotion	6.9
4.4	Representational Functions	0.1
4.5	Promotion of Interest of the Local Community	1.5
4.6	Twinning of Local Authority Areas	0.2
4.8	Administration and Miscellaneous	10.5
Less:	Inter-Authority Contributions	0.8
TOTAL		**36.9**
5.	**Environmental Protection**	**£m**
5.1	Waste Disposal	68.1
5.2	Burial Grounds	5.6
5.3	Safety of Structures/Places	6.0

5.4	Fire Protection	84.0
5.5	Pollution Control	5.4
5.8	Administration and Miscellaneous	18.3
Less:	Inter-Authority Contributions	18.7

TOTAL		**168.7**

6.	**Recreation and Amenity**	**£m**
6.1	Swimming Pools	7.6
6.2	Libraries	32.6
6.3	Parks, Open Spaces, Recreation Centres etc.	64.4
6.4	Other Recreation and Amenity	22.5
6.8	Administration and Miscellaneous	11.6
Less:	Inter-Authority Contributions	2.6

TOTAL		**136.1**

7.	**Agriculture, Education, Health & Welfare**	**£m**
7.1	Agriculture	5.1
7.2	Education	96.4
7.3	Health and Welfare	0.8
7.8	Administration and Miscellaneous	6.5
Less:	Inter-Authority Contributions	0.7

TOTAL		**108.1**

8.	**Miscellaneous Services**	**£m**
8.1	Land Acquisition	1.1
8.2	Plant and Materials	0.2
8.3	Financial Management	21.4
8.4	Elections	2.1
8.5	Administration of Justice and Consumer Protection	8.8
8.6	Property Damage	2.0
8.7	Markets, Fairs and Abattoirs	1.4
8.8	Administration and Miscellaneous	26.7
8.9	Chairman's Allowance	0.5
8.10	Entertainment and Associated Expenses	0.4
8.11	Expenses of Members and Representation at Conferences	4.6
8.12	Expenses of Members Attending Conferences Abroad	0.4
Less:	Inter-Authority Contributions	2.0

TOTAL		**67.6**

ALL PROGRAMME GROUPS TOTAL	**1126.3**

Source: Department of the Environment, *Local Authority Estimates 1995.*

- a grant paid by the National Roads Authority (which is in turn funded by the Department of the Environment) for the management and maintenance of national roads (1995 – £23 million);
- grants paid by the Department of the Environment for the management and maintenance of non-national roads (in the form of block grants) and also grants under the restoration programme which commenced in 1995 (1995-£28 million);
- a grant paid by the Department of Education in respect of VEC superannuation costs (1995 – £18 million);
- a grant paid by the Department of the Environment to meet the cost of motor tax collection, driver licensing and vehicle testing (1995 – £12 million).[11]

Total current central government grants amounted to an estimated £404 million in 1995. Grants are discussed further in chapter 7.

Miscellaneous receipts (also known as goods and services income) come from a wide variety of sources including:

- housing loan repayments by house purchasers or by those who borrowed from local authorities to improve houses (1995 – £112 million);
- rents from local authority houses (1995 – £64 million);
- charges for domestic water supply, refuse and sewerage services (1995 – £46 million, £7 million and £2 million respectively);
- commercial/industrial water charges (1995 – £39 million);
- tenant purchase payments (1995 – £17 million),;
- planning application fees (1995 – £7 million);
- commercial refuse charges (1995 – £7 million);
- swimming pool fees (1995 – £4 million);
- library fees (1995 – £1 million).

These receipts also amounted to an estimated £404 million in 1995. The issue of charging for services is discussed in chapter 8.

Local authorities now rely on rates for 28 per cent of current income, on grants for 36 per cent and on miscellaneous receipts for 36 per cent. Table 5 sets out changes in the relative sources of local authority income since 1973. There are two major trends to be observed from the table. The first concerns the period 1973-83, when there was a shift in the burden of financing local expenditure of some 30 per cent from local rates to central government grants. This largely reflected the progressive reduction, followed by the ending, of rates on domestic property and agricultural land, and their replacement by grants paid by central government to local authorities and financed out of general taxation.

The second feature relates to the period 1983-95 and appears to indicate a substantial reversal of the earlier trend, with a greater proportion of local expenditure being met out of local sources, rather than central government grants. In general, what happened in these years was that central government subsidies to meet (in whole or in part) local authority loan repayments on capital borrowings were ended, and a series of deductions was made from RSG, to counterbalance the removal from local authorities of liability for such repayments and for certain other items of expenditure. These changes were made in the interests of rationalising public financial procedures (including introducing 100 per cent central government funding for some local capital programmes) and ending local authority responsibility for expenditure which was no longer appropriate to them; the technical effect was to reduce substantially the level of local current ex-

Table 5: Sources of Local Authority Current Income 1973–95

	Rates %	Central Government Grants %	Miscellaneous Receipts %
1973	42	38	20
1983	12	67	21
1995	28	36	36

Sources: Department of the Environment, *Returns of Local Taxation 1973* and *1983*; and *Local Authority Estimates 1995* (adjusted to exclude central government non-national road improvement grants).

penditure and to increase the proportion of such expenditure financed by local sources rather than by central government grants.[12] In addition, leaving aside these adjustments, the level of increases in RSG (and its predecessors) over the years was limited by central government as part of its efforts to correct imbalances in the public finances, with reductions in the level of grant occurring in 1987-89; other things being equal, this would have had an effect on the proportionate sources of income. Finally, national road grants were treated as a capital, not a current, item from 1993 onwards.

Table 6 highlights the relative dependence of county councils – the principal unit of local government outside the main cities – on central government. The counties do not have extensive built-up areas from which income can be raised via commercial/ industrial rates and domestic service charges. However, in the context of proposals to extend town boundaries to include adjoining county areas into which towns have expanded, consideration is given to compensating county councils for loss of part of the local revenue-raising capacity which they do have, and financial adjustments are often made between the local authorities concerned.

Figure 2 summarises the sources of local government finance (current and capital).

Figure 2: Sources of Local Government Finance

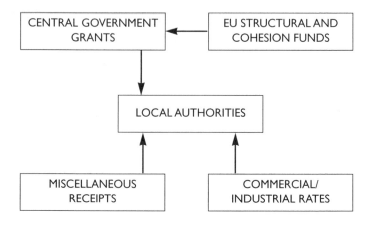

Table 6: Sources of Estimated Current Income by Type of Local Authority, 1995

	Rates %	Central Government Grants %	Miscellaneous Receipts %
County Councils	21	43	36
County Borough Corporations	42	23	35
Borough Corporations/ Urban District Councils	45	20	35

Source: Department of the Environment, *Local Authority Estimates 1995* (adjusted to exclude central government non-national road improvement grants).

International Comparisons

How does Ireland compare with other countries in relation to sources of local government finance? This issue is difficult to address due to problems in obtaining reliable, comparable and up-to-date data. These problems are compounded by the fact that the structure of local government finance is under regular review and subject to change in many countries.

Table 7 sets out percentage sources of local government finance (current and capital) using OECD data for a number of federal and unitary developed countries. Dealing first with the level of reliance on central government grants, the table shows large variations between, for example, Italy where 83 per cent of local government finance comes from the centre, and Sweden where the comparable figure is 20 per cent. As regards income from local taxes, there is again a large variation – from the Netherlands at 6 per cent to Sweden at 65 per cent.

Ireland varies significantly from the average on both criteria: 51 per cent of total local authority finance here (current and capital) comes from central government grants compared to the unweighted mean of 38 per cent, and 17 per cent is derived from local taxes as against the unweighted mean of 42 per cent. There also appears to be greater reliance in Ireland on sources of finance other than grants and taxes: 32 per cent versus 20 per cent.

Table 7: Sources of Finance for State and Local Authorities in Federal and Unitary OECD Countries as % of Total Finance (Current and Capital)

Country	Level	Year	State/ Local Taxes	Central Government Grants	Other
Australia	State	1990	33	44	23
	Local	1990	43	17	40
Austria	State	1990	49	37	14
	Local	1990	52	16	32
Belgium	Local	1989	35	56	9
Canada	State	1989	66	21	13
	Local	1989	40	45	15
Denmark	Local	1990	47	43	10
Finland	Local	1989	47	34	19
France	Local	1990	44	35	21
Germany	State	1990	71	16	13
	Local	1990	36	27	37
Ireland	Local	1995	17	51	32
Italy	Local	1989	7	83	10
Netherlands	Local	1990	6	80	14
Norway	Local	1990	47	40	13
Spain	Local	1989	57	26	17
Sweden	Local	1989	65	20	15
United Kingdom	Local	1989	33	43	24
United States	State	1989	54	20	26
	Local	1989	40	38	22
Unweighted mean			42	38	20

Sources: Ireland – Tables 3 and 5. Other countries – *Revenue Statistics of OECD Member Countries 1965-1991*, Paris: OECD (1992), country tables at pages 205-253. 'State authorities' refer to intermediate units of government in federal countries and 'state taxes' to taxes accruing to such units.

Ireland comes closer to the average for grants, but not for local taxes or other sources, when comparison is made with other small unitary European countries – Belgium, Denmark, Finland, the Netherlands, Norway and Sweden. The unweighted mean for these countries plus Ireland is 46 per cent grants, 38 per cent local taxes and 16 per cent other sources.

Care must be taken, however, lest an overly simplistic view be taken from these data. In other European countries there are complex arrangements governing responsibility for the levying, collecting and use of the proceeds of taxes between different levels of government which make it difficult to distinguish clearly between 'central' and 'state' or 'local' taxes. In particular, OECD data treat as state or local taxes instruments under which state or local authorities, despite having wide-ranging functions in many cases, have little or no discretion over the rate of taxation and often do not even collect the tax themselves.[13] Examples of countries with such taxes are:

- Germany, where 15 per cent of the revenue from federal income taxes is shared with local authorities; this source constituted over 42 per cent of the total tax revenue of the lowest tier of local government (*Gemeiden*) in 1990;
- The United Kingdom, where from 1986-87 central government 'capped' the rates being levied by what were seen as high-spending local authorities prior to the abolition of domestic rates in 1990 and their replacement by the community charge or poll tax. Today commercial/industrial rates are set nationally (the uniform business rate) and, in fact, only around 16 per cent of council spending is met through the one locally-decided tax, the council tax. Furthermore, Whitehall retains and continues to use the power to cap local budgets deemed to be excessive;
- Norway, where Parliament decides a ceiling for local income tax rates that every municipality and county uses in practice – local income tax being the main source of local finance;
- Sweden, where central government imposed a freeze on local tax rates in 1990;
- Spain, where local tax rates are levied within limits set by central government.[14]

In contrast, the data for Ireland include only a tax in respect of which local authorities have complete discretion (commercial/industrial rates).

Table 8 details the yield from state and local taxes in a number of OECD countries as a percentage of GDP. Firstly, it illustrates the importance of income taxes as a source of local government finance – such taxes are used in twelve out of sixteen of the countries covered. Secondly, only in Ireland (and the United Kingdom more recently than indicated in the table, with the replacement of the poll tax by the council tax) is local taxation confined to one particular category of tax. In some countries at least four forms of taxation are used by local authorities even

Table 8: Yields of State and Local Taxes in Federal and Unitary OECD Countries as % of GDP, 1990

Country	Income Taxes	Property Taxes	Sales Taxes	Other Taxes	Total
Sweden	17.9	–	0.1	–	18.0
Canada	6.8	3.4	4.6	1.9	16.7
Denmark	14.4	1.1	–	–	15.5
Germany	7.8	1.2	2.5	0.4	11.9
Finland	10.9	0.1	–	–	11.0
Norway	9.0	0.9	–	0.4	10.3
United States	2.5	3.1	3.4	0.7	9.7
Austria	4.3	0.4	3.6	1.4	9.7
Australia	–	2.7	0.7	2.9	6.3
Spain	0.8	2.0	1.3	0.7	4.8
France	0.5	1.5	0.2	1.9	4.1
United Kingdom★	–	0.6	–	1.7	2.3
Belgium	1.6	–	–	0.2	1.8
Italy	0.7	–	0.2	0.4	1.3
Netherlands	–	0.8	–	0.3	1.1
Ireland (1995)	–	0.8	–	–	0.8
Unweighted mean	4.8	1.2	1.0	0.8	7.8

Sources: Ireland – Department of the Environment, *Local Authority Estimates 1995* and Central Bank, *Annual Report 1994.* Other countries – *Revenue Statistics of OECD Member Countries 1965-1991*, Paris: OECD (1992), Tables 125 and 127. 'State taxes' mean taxes accruing to intermediate units of government in federal countries.

★*Note:* Since 1990, the council tax has replaced the poll tax in the United Kingdom - the council tax is a hybrid tax based mainly on the capital value of domestic property but modulated according to size of household and with rebates for those on low income. The local taxes in that country (the uniform business rate and the council tax) should now more properly be included in the 'Property Taxes' column only.

though some of those may be of little consequence. On the other hand, it may be argued that the use of a single form of taxation enhances transparency and accountability, objectives which may not be served by more complex taxation arrangements. Thirdly, arising from the limited functions of Irish local authorities and the below-average reliance on local taxes for a given level of local expenditure, the yield from Irish local taxes as a percentage of GDP – at 0.8 per cent – is very low compared to the unweighted mean of 7.8 per cent. As a percentage of GNP in Ireland, the yield is 0.9 per cent.

Two other points are worth noting. As suggested above, 'An important aspect of European local finance is the prevalence of revenue-sharing schemes by which part of the proceeds from one or several national taxes is assigned to local government'.[15] Furthermore, central government grants (including assigned revenues) are commonly distributed according to criteria measuring differences in the needs and resources of local authority areas. 'In most European countries, in the United States, Canada and Australia, equalisation has been made an explicit objective of the grant system'.[16]

Council of Europe Charter of Local Self-Government

This Charter, which was adopted in 1985, attempts to set out principles for protecting and strengthening local autonomy in Europe. Article 9, on the financial resources of local authorities, reads as follows:

1. Local authorities shall be entitled, within national economic policy, to adequate financial resources of their own, of which they may dispose freely within the framework of their powers.
2. Local authorities' financial resources shall be commensurate with the responsibilities provided for by the constitution and the law.
3. Part at least of the financial resources of local authorities shall derive from local taxes and charges of which, within the limits of statute, they have the power to determine the rate.

4. The financial systems on which resources available to local authorities are based shall be of a sufficiently diversified and buoyant nature to enable them to keep pace as far as practically possible with the real evolution of the cost of carrying out their tasks.

5. The protection of financially weaker local authorities calls for the institution of financial equalisation procedures or equivalent measures which are designed to correct the effects of the unequal distribution of potential sources of finance and of the financial burden they must support. Such procedures or measures shall not diminish the discretion local authorities may exercise within their own sphere of responsibility.

6. Local authorities shall be consulted, in an appropriate manner, on the way in which redistributed resources are to be allocated to them.

7. As far as possible, grants to local authorities shall not be earmarked for the financing of specific projects. The provision of grants shall not remove the basic freedom of local authorities to exercise policy discretion within their own jurisdiction.

8. For the purpose of borrowing for capital investment, local authorities shall have access to the national capital market within the limits of the law.

The article illustrates well the concerns of European local authorities in relation to financial resources; these include adequacy of funding, freedom as to purposes of expenditure, access to and power to decide rates of local taxation and charges, equalisation, and use of general rather than specific grants. It also contains qualifications which reflect concerns of central governments, such as conformity with national economic policy, possible limits on local taxation powers and recognition that it will not always be feasible to avoid the use of grants for specific projects.

Macroeconomic Context

Local government finance cannot be viewed in isolation from national economic developments; in particular it must be seen in the context of the total system of national taxation and public expenditure.

Total Tax Burden
The ratio of tax/GDP rose from 31 per cent in the late 1970s to 39 per cent in the mid–1980s, at a rate of three times the OECD average. Since 1985 tighter public expenditure control, faster GDP growth and lower interest rates first allowed the tax/GDP ratio to stabilise (between 1985 and 1987) and eventually, after a temporary increase linked to the 1988 tax amnesty, to fall. The tax/GDP ratio was about 37 per cent in 1994, which was lower than the EU and OECD averages.

However, two points need to be made. First, a better indication of tax burden is the ratio of tax to GNP rather than GDP. For most countries this makes little difference. However, in Ireland, because of interest payments on foreign debt and repatriated profits, national income (or GNP) is significantly lower than GDP.[17] As a ratio of GNP, the tax burden in Ireland is higher at over 40 per cent. Secondly, the level of income per head of the OECD countries with which we are normally compared is significantly higher than in Ireland; our *per capita* income is about three-fifths of the OECD average.

Against this background it is easy to understand public resistance to new taxes and to increases in existing taxes. This suggests that if there is to be increased reliance on local taxation, it may have to be offset by reductions in central government grants to local authorities, thereby allowing a reduction in national taxes. It also implies that it may not be feasible to increase national taxes significantly in order to provide substantially higher central government grants to local authorities or indeed to other public bodies funded by the Exchequer.

Fiscal Policy
An important driver of fiscal policy up to the year 2000 will be the national policy objective of qualifying for EMU under the provisions of the Maastricht Treaty. It is arguable, however, that

even without this Treaty obligation the desirability of reducing the Irish debt burden would require similar policies.

Debt reduction can release significant resources for public expenditure increases and tax reductions in the medium term. For example, the reduction in the proportion of national income going to debt service, from 11.1 per cent of GNP in 1985 to 7.8 per cent in 1993, is now (1995) worth the equivalent of £1.1 billion per annum. Debt reduction can be a very good investment which pays significant dividends over a relatively short timescale.

The Maastricht Treaty provides that fiscal policy will continue mainly to be decided at national level, while monetary policy decisions will be made at EU level.[18] The Treaty specifies two fiscal rules which must be met if a country is to qualify for the third stage of EMU:

- a general government deficit of less than 3 per cent of GDP ('unless either the ratio has declined substantially and continuously and reached a level that comes close to' 3 per cent or 'The excess ... is only exceptional and temporary');
- a debt/GDP ratio of less than 60 per cent – or if above that level, approaching it at a satisfactory pace.

Maastricht provides a context and a discipline which it seems likely will govern the management of Ireland's public finances over the next decade. These disciplines will also affect the financing of local authorities and other public bodies. In 1995 the level of the general government deficit was 2.1 per cent of GDP and the debt ratio was 85 per cent of GDP.[19] Ireland meets the current deficit criterion now; the debt ratio is considerably above the Maastricht target but nevertheless represents substantial progress since 1987, when the figure was 116 per cent.

To help to ensure that Ireland meets the Maastricht criteria, the Government has adopted a limit on current supply services spending of 2 per cent plus inflation for 1996 and 1997.[20] This will require a more restrictive approach to public spending than has been achieved over the last five years. If there are to be significant increases in Exchequer-financed local authority expenditure, or in any other expenditure area, these will have to be accommodated by reductions in other areas of spending or by increases in taxation. Both of these possibilities appear difficult to achieve and it seems unlikely that any sector will be exempt from the fiscal discipline implied by the Maastricht Treaty for the remainder of the decade and beyond.

Tax Competition
An important constraint on the level of taxation in Ireland is the need to maintain the overall competitiveness of the economy. Taxation is but one element of competition in an increasingly competitive world. There is evidence of a worldwide downward movement in personal and company tax rates and there has also been some reduction in VAT rates and withholding tax on interest within the EU.[21] However, EU Governments have taken steps to limit tax competition by adopting minimum rates or levels for the main indirect taxes.

In setting tax rates, countries increasingly have to take account of the levels of taxation imposed in other competing countries, particularly where the activity or factor involved is mobile. These constraints are also relevant for local taxation.

Conclusion

This chapter has shown the relatively confined remit of local government in Ireland: local authorities are concerned mainly with housing, roads, water and sewerage services, physical planning and environmental protection, together with a range of other smaller-scale functions. Central government is the principal source of finance for local capital expenditure; miscellaneous receipts, central government grants and commercial/industrial rates are the sources of finance for spending on current account.

By international standards, Ireland appears to rely to a greater extent on central government grants and miscellaneous receipts than on local taxes, but the situation is complicated by restrictions on local taxation powers in other countries. Future spending by local authorities (and other public bodies) is likely to be constrained by the relatively high tax burden in Ireland and the need to control borrowing and spending to meet obligations under the Maastricht Treaty and the expectations of financial markets.

NOTES TO CHAPTER 2

1. Department of the Environment, *Local Authority Estimates 1995*, Dublin: Stationery Office (1995). Total 'current' expenditure of £1224 million in that volume is reduced by £98 million in respect of expenditure on non-national road improvement. Such expenditure is by convention included in local authority current estimates and accounts but is treated in this text as a capital item. See also Table 3

2. Department of Finance, *Budget Book 1995;* Department of the Environment, *Local Authority Estimates 1995*; Central Bank, *Annual Report 1994*

3. The establishment of the Environmental Protection Agency under the Environmental Protection Agency Act, 1992 has removed from local authorities responsibility for licensing activities with potential for significant environmental damage

4. *Report of Advisory Expert Committee on Local Government Reorganisation and Reform*, Dublin: Stationery Office (1991), p. 19

5. G. Danaher, 'Financing Local Government: The Irish System and Options for the Future', in *The Financing of Local Government,* Dublin: Foundation for Fiscal Studies (1991), p. 31

6. For an up-to-date account of local development agencies see *Operational Programme for Local Urban and Rural Development 1994-1999*, Dublin : Stationery Office (1995). For a sceptical view of the desirability of the extension of the local authority role in this area see NESC, *New Approaches to Rural Development*, Dublin: NESC (1994), pp. 134-39

7. Department of the Environment, Press Releases, 26 July 1995 and 5 February 1996

8. Industry does in some instances make capital contributions where facilities serve its needs. For a relevant recent study see ESRI, *Waste*

Water Services: Charging Industry the Capital Cost, Dublin: ESRI (1994)

9. Department of the Environment, *Environment Bulletin*, Issue No. 27, August 1995, p. 16

10. Department of the Environment, *Local Authority Estimates 1995*, Dublin: Stationery Office (1995)

11. Changes are being introduced in 1996 which will eliminate the need for this grant by allowing these expenses of local authorities to be deducted from motor tax collected locally: *Official Report of Dail Debates* 23 January 1996, Question No. 240

12. The following were the principal changes: the supplementary welfare allowance demand payable to health boards was removed in 1986; required payments to the Office of Public Works relating to arterial drainage and to ACOT ended in 1987 and 1988 respectively; local authority liability to make certain loan repayments to the Local Loans Fund ceased in 1988 when 100 per cent grants were introduced for some local capital programmes (e.g. water and sewerage services); the ESB began to pay rates directly to local authorities rather than through RSG in 1989; the costs in meeting VEC pensions were removed in 1990; and the levy on local authorities in respect of the Local Appointments Commission ended in 1995. In terms of effects on the proportionate sources of income, the Local Loans Fund changes were the most significant

13. *Revenue Statistics of OECD Member Countries, 1965-1991,* Paris: OECD (1992), pp. 44-5

14. R. Bennett and G. Krebs, 'Local Government Finance in Germany'; J. Gibson, 'Local Government Finance under the Conservatives'; L. Oulasvirta, 'Municipal Public Finance in the Nordic Countries'; and A. Santigosa, 'The Finance of Spanish Local Government and its Recent Reform', *Local Government Studies*, Winter 1993. See also *The Economist*, 7 May 1994, p. 40

15. Institute for Fiscal Studies, 'Report on the Role of Central Grants in Local Finance in the Republic of Ireland', printed as supplement to *Report of Advisory Expert Committee, op.cit.,* p. 13

16. NESC, *The Financing of Local Authorities,* Dublin: NESC (1985), page 88. See also P. Blair, 'Financial Equalisation between Local and Regional Authorities in European Countries', *Local Government Studies*, Winter 1993

17. GNP in Ireland in 1994 was 88 per cent of GDP. Central Bank, *Annual Report 1994*

18. *Treaty on European Union (Maastricht Treaty)*, Official Journal of the European Communities, C224 Volume 35, 31 August 1992

19. Department of Finance, *Economic Background to the 1996 Budget*

20. *Policy Agreement, A Government of Renewal*, Dublin: (1995), p. 11. At the time of writing it appeared that the 2 per cent limit would be exceeded for 1996, but this does not alter the essential thrust of the argument in the text

21. *Report of the Committee of Independent Experts on Company Taxation* (Ruding Committee), Brussels: Commission of the European Communities (1992)

3
CENTRAL-LOCAL RELATIONS

Introduction
The financial links between central and local authorities should in theory reflect society's view on an appropriate distribution of power between the two levels of government. If there is no detailed consideration of the proper balance between the central and the local, there is a risk that financial arrangements of themselves will determine where that balance lies. This chapter outlines one theoretical approach to central-local relations – the distinction between national and local services – and introduces the concept of subsidiarity. It also describes two critical aspects of that relationship (the EU dimension and audit/value for money issues) and attempts to summarise where the balance lies at present in central-local relations. Finally, reference is made to the recommendations for change contained in the Barrington Report.

National and Local Services
Economic justifications for government spending in a market economy focus largely on the concepts of public goods and merit goods. In welfare economics, a public good is a good which, even if consumed by one person, can still be consumed by other people.[1] Widespread public benefits from the provision of such goods – would-be producers cannot prevent benefits accruing to consumers who refuse to pay – mean that private markets will not produce the socially-efficient quantity; hence the justification for government spending. Examples of public goods are defence, clean air and street cleaning.

A merit good is a good that society thinks everyone ought to have regardless of whether it is wanted by each individual.[2]

Society may value such goods, and provide them at a higher quantity and at a lower or no cost compared to what would occur in a free market, because of benefits from their provision which extend beyond individuals to others in society or because it makes a judgment as to what is in the best interest of the individual. Examples of merit goods are education, health and housing.

Apart from these essentially economic justifications for government spending, a further important role for government lies in the promotion of social equity through income transfers to, and expenditure programmes targeted on, the less well-off. In terms of local public finance theory, the question to be addressed is which public services are to be controlled nationally (though administered locally) and which are to be determined at local level.

National services are those undertaken by local authorities on behalf of central government; uniform principles for their administration are laid down by the central authority. Economic efficiency arguments in favour of the determination of particular services on a national scale often relate to benefits from the services accruing to people living outside the local authority area – externalities. An externality arises whenever an individual's production or consumption decision directly affects the production or consumption of others other than through market prices.[3] The concept may also be applied to local authority decisions. Take the example of a motorway through county A on the road to city B; much of the benefit of such a service will accrue to people other than the residents of county A. If the provision of such a service is left entirely to the discretion of county A (particularly if it is to be financed by them by local taxation), there will be a misallocation of resources in that the motorway will be built much later and to a much lower standard than if there is a national specification and the cost is borne from central taxation. This analysis can also be applied on a multinational level and it provides part of the justification for EU funding of infrastructural projects in member states.

A second efficiency argument for national services concerns

possible economies of scale to be derived from providing certain services in respect of units larger than the conventional local authority areas. Both of these factors – externalities and economies of scale – would not normally be taken into account by local authorities in their decision-making and can be used to justify central government intervention in the provision of certain services.

In addition to the traditional concern of economic theory with efficiency, there may also be equity justifications for national level services. These may include a need to secure uniformity in the standard of a service: it may be considered that a service is of such importance to individual welfare that it would be inequitable to permit significant local variation in its provision. Similarly, equity considerations may point to reliefs from local taxes and charges for lower income groups and to central government meeting the cost, in keeping with the principles underlying national social welfare systems.

Local services are optional to a large degree in that the locality has wide discretion as to the extent to which, and the manner in which, the services are provided. With local services, there is great scope for local variety and initiative and they can with benefit be made the responsibility of the local authority and the local community.

Theoretical arguments in favour of decentralised decision-making and local provision and financing of services comprise a set of concepts which together are commonly referred to as 'fiscal federalism.'[4] An important aspect of this approach is the assumption that the role of local government is to provide services in varying ways and levels in accordance with the differing wishes of people in different parts of a country. Local authorities have greater information about local needs and so allocative efficiency is served by allowing them to provide the mix of services that most closely reflects these preferences; inefficiency arises if the same output is provided when variations are desired by recipients and there are no compensating advantages from national control.

Further advantages of decentralisation are seen to be the competition which is likely to arise between neighbouring local authorities over the mix of services provided, and the capacity of smaller units to produce more innovative policies. Finally, problems can be settled earlier if they can be decided locally rather than if they have to be decided nationally. If too much has to be referred to the centre, decision-making may become overloaded at that level and decisions may be delayed giving rise to efficiency losses.

Political, as opposed to economic, arguments for local decision-making reflect belief in the importance to the democratic process of the dispersal of power throughout society and of the widest possible participation in public decision-making. On this view, local government is one of the essential elements of democracy, allowing local issues to be settled by local people or their representatives, and local communities to take ownership of governmental decisions affecting their lives.

In the provision of national services, which may be financed primarily if not wholly from central taxation using specific grants, local authorities may be seen as the implementation agents of central government. There may be some areas of discretion where central government is undecided, or chooses not to intervene, but all such discretion is subject to national control. In the provision of local services, local authorities would have complete freedom and discretion in both policy and administration. Local services (as defined above) can be financed in three main ways:

- local taxes, which would give local authorities discretion as to the level and mix of local services;
- general central government grants, which would give local authorities discretion over the mix of local services but would automatically carry a limit on the overall level of expenditure on such services;
- a combination of local taxes and general central government grants.

In practice, it may not be clear whether services are suitable for market or government provision; and services can contain both national and local elements (which might call for specific grants to meet only part of the cost). In addition, the character of services may change over time. These factors create difficulties in determining the role of government, the level of government at which particular services should be decided, and the means by which they should be financed.

Subsidiarity

The principle of subsidiarity has often been used in discussions of central-local relations – in particular by advocates of local determination and provision of services. It comes from Catholic social teaching and means that functions should be carried out at the level closest to the individual, and only carried out at a higher level when they effectively cannot be carried out at the lower level. It was last restated in a papal encyclical, *Quadragesimo Anno*, in 1941: 'It is an injustice, a grave evil, and a disturbance of the right order for a large and higher organisation to arrogate to itself functions which can be performed efficiently by smaller and lower bodies'.[5] This principle is embodied, in more measured terms, in the Council of Europe Charter of Local Self-Government which states: 'Public responsibilities shall generally be exercised, in preference, by those authorities which are closest to the citizen. Allocation of responsibility to another authority should weigh up the extent and nature of the task and the requirements of efficiency and economy' (Article 4.3). A recent official definition of subsidiarity is that 'public services (should) be devolved to the level nearest those to whom the service is delivered, but with due regard to financial constraints, efficiency and staffing implications'.[6]

The issue has also arisen at EU level. In a report in 1993 to the European Council on the 'Adaptation of Community Legislation to the Subsidiarity Principle', the European Commission stated that 'the aim of subsidiarity is to see to it that decisions are taken as close as possible to the citizen, a constant watch being kept to ensure that action taken at Community level is justified in the light of the means available to national, regional or local authorities'. In the Commission's view, application of the subsidiarity principle has the following consequences for the EU:

- EU competence is not the rule but rather an exception to national competence; in other words, the EU must have powers specifically conferred on it before action can be taken;
- far from having the effect of freezing EU action, the dynamic of the subsidiarity principle should make it possible to expand it if required, or limit or even abandon it when action at EU level is no longer warranted;
- the regulatory role of subsidiarity, for which need for action is the criterion, applies to shared competence only; it cannot be used as a pretext for challenging measures in areas such as the internal market where the EU has a clearly defined and undeniable obligation to act.[7]

The Maastricht Treaty adds the requirement that each EU proposal, whether in the realm of exclusive or shared competence, must respect the principle of proportionality. The intensity of the action should leave the member states all possible room for manoeuvre in its implementation. Subsidiarity requires EU legislation to be limited to what is essential.

EU Dimension

Membership of the EU affects virtually all aspects of Irish public life and local government finance is no exception. It is possible to identify at least three ways in which the widening and (sometimes) deepening Union impinges on local government finance: through the level of local public expenditure, the purposes of such expenditure and the procedures followed in the expenditure process.

While the original Treaty of Rome made no provision for a regional policy, the Preamble to the Treaty declared the anxiety of the parties to secure the reduction of differences in regional development, and the European Social Fund (ESF) and European Agriculture Guidance and Guarantee Fund (EAGGF) (FEOGA in French) operated from the early years of the Community. It was not, however, until the establishment of the ERDF in 1975 that a formal Community regional policy emerged. The effectiveness of early Community regional policy was, nevertheless, limited due, *inter alia*, to the small proportion of the Community budget devoted to it.[8]

Revisions to the Treaty of Rome effected by the Single European Act in 1987 reformed Community regional policy in a fundamental way. The Act stipulated that the Community would aim at reducing disparities between regions (new Article 130A of the Treaty); it was accompanied by measures to increase substantially the level of regional aid and to make regional policy more effective. This enhanced emphasis on regional policy was prompted by recognition of the advantages to the core, wealthier countries of the realisation in 1992 of a Single Market in goods and services. In the absence of large-scale fiscal transfers, it was possible that peripheral, 'cohesion' countries could fall further behind countries closer to the heart of the Single Market. Under the reformed Structural Funds (the ERDF, ESF and EAGGF), priority was to be given to areas where the GDP *per capita* was less than 75 per cent of the Community norm. Such areas were termed Objective 1 regions, and the policy was to promote the development and structural adjustment of regions whose development was lagging behind.

The Maastricht Treaty of 1993 commenced a process of wider economic and monetary integration within the European Union (as it now became) and was also accompanied by increased commitment to, and funding for, regional policy. In particular, a new Cohesion Fund, confined to member states where GNP *per capita* was less than 90 per cent of the EU average (i.e. Ireland, Spain, Portugal and Greece), was established to finance projects in the fields of environmental protection and transport networks. It is additional to the three Structural Funds proper – the ERDF, the ESF and the EAGGF.

Ireland's GDP *per capita* was 62 per cent of the Community average in 1988.[9] This country has, therefore, been a major beneficiary from European Structural and Cohesion Funds in recent years. The amount of public expenditure in Ireland financed in this way increased from £340 million in 1988 to an average of £660 million per annum in 1989–93 and was projected to rise to about £1 billion per annum in 1994–99.[10]

These funds are not, however, made available in block form to be disbursed in whatever manner may be decided nationally, although it has been argued that they should be so that, for example, they could be applied to reduce the national debt.[11] Rather, the funds are provided for specific purposes agreed in partnership with the European Commission and in accordance with the terms of EU Regulations. The principal local expenditure programmes financed in part by the EU are:

- the national primary road network, which accounts for less than 3 per cent of total road mileage but carries 27 per cent of all traffic;[12]
- the national secondary road network, which accounts for 3 per cent of total road mileage and 11 per cent of traffic;
- non-national roads of particular importance to identified economic sectors;
- traffic management measures in the area covered by the Dublin Transportation Initiative;
- water supply and sewerage facilities;
- works to promote renewal of the urban and village environment;
- waste recovery facilities;
- works carried out as part of Community Employment.

In general, EU funds finance capital expenditure which is likely to enhance economic development. Thus social housing, directly concerned as it is with social equity rather than economic efficiency, does not generally qualify for such funding.

While EU funding has increased the overall level of resources available for local expenditure, and directed resources to particular programmes, it has also affected the procedures involved in the expenditure process. Since the foundation of the EU regional policy, Ireland has been treated as a single region for this purpose, and control of resources from the Structural Funds and the Cohesion Fund lies mostly with central government to which funds of benefit to local authorities are generally remitted by Brussels. Local authorities benefit by means of grants from central government which are partly recouped by the EU (usually the ERDF or the Cohesion Fund but also on occasion the ESF and EAGGF), with the balance being met by the Exchequer itself; on occasion, central government grants are fully financed by the EU.

The general practice of central government control would seem to mean that EU assistance does not make much difference in procedural terms to local authorities. However, finance from the Structural Funds involves an extensive expenditure planning, monitoring, and evaluation process which includes:

- preparation by central government of a National Development Plan setting out a proposed strategy for utilisation of the funds;
- negotiation with the European Commission of a Community Support Framework containing an agreement on the funding of particular programmes over the planning period;
- preparation by Government Departments of operational programmes setting out strategy in each sector (e.g. transport, environmental services, local urban and rural development, human resources development);
- negotiation and agreement of operational programmes with the European Commission taking account of national and EU priorities;
- evaluation and selection of projects to receive funding over the period;
- monitoring and review to ensure that objectives are achieved.

Under the Community Support Framework for 1994-1999, the following local expenditure programmes are being grant-aided:

- investment in national primary and secondary roads, non-national roads of economic importance and traffic management measures under the Dublin Transportation Initiative (Operational Programme for Transport; ERDF);
- provision of water supply, sewerage and waste recovery

facilities (Operational Programme for Environmental Services; ERDF);

- the carrying out of urban and village renewal works (Operational Programme for Local Urban and Rural Development; ERDF and EAGGF); and
- works carried out as part of Community Employment (Operational Programme for Human Resource Development; ESF).

While central government has the lead role in the expenditure planning process, local authorities are also involved. Firstly, the eight regional authorities established by the Minister for the Environment on 1 January 1994 under the Local Government Act, 1991, to promote the coordination of the provision of public services in their areas, also provide an input to the preparation of proposals for EU funding and monitor progress on EU-assisted measures in the various regions. Membership of the authorities consists of councillors nominated by local authorities in the region and each authority is assisted in its functions by an operational committee which includes relevant local authority officials and, for EU purposes, representatives from the social partners, voluntary groups, Government departments and the European Commission. In performing EU-related functions, regional authorities replaced sub-regional review committees which had carried out this work in earlier years.

Secondly, local authorities are represented where appropriate on the monitoring committees set up to oversee implementation of each operational programme. Finally, as the bodies responsible for implementation of many EU-assisted projects, local authorities need to comply with specific EU information requirements covering areas such as project evaluation prior to commencement, progress reports on works as they proceed, and audit/evaluation of completed schemes. This information is provided by local authorities to the European Commission via the Department of the Environment.

The Cohesion Fund operates differently from the Structural Funds in that it functions on a project-by-project basis, and the rate of EU aid can be as high as 85 per cent compared to 75 per cent in the case of the Structural Funds proper. It also, however, involves extensive planning, evaluation and monitoring procedures. The Cohesion Fund finances investment in national primary roads, water supply and sewerage facilities and waste infrastructure.[13]

A limited amount (9 per cent) of the Structural Funds is devoted to Community Initiatives which are not restricted to national governments and can also be availed of by local authorities, semi-state bodies and voluntary groups. These initiatives are administered by the European Commission in accordance with special needs which it identifies. Their aim is to secure added value over the rest of the Structural Funds by focusing on measures which involve cooperation between border areas, innovative approaches to development, local participation, etc. They also involve significant planning, evaluation and monitoring procedures, including the preparation of operational programmes. In general, initiatives embrace a wide range of measures in a package designed to tackle problems in a comprehensive way. Among the initiatives which include measures of relevance to local government in Ireland are:

- INTERREG, which focuses on cross-border cooperation and development between Ireland and Northern Ireland and between Ireland and Wales. Non-national road improvements, water supply/sewerage facilities and other environmental measures are financed between Ireland and Northern Ireland; roads (national and non-national) are the main local authority focus of the initiative as it affects Ireland and Wales. The ERDF finances these works;
- The Special Support Programme for Peace and Reconciliation in Northern Ireland and the Border Counties of Ireland. Urban and village renewal, roads and small-scale environmental infrastructure benefit from this initiative and these are financed by the ERDF and the EAGGF;
- LEADER, which finances local action groups, operating

outside the formal local government system, to implement plans for integrated rural development.[14]

Audit/Value for Money

In addition to systems of internal audit, expenditure by local authorities is also controlled by a system under which the accounts of each authority must be audited by a local government auditor appointed by the Minister for the Environment. Individual local government auditors are 'statutorily independent but administratively they are officers of the Department of the Environment.'[15]

Statutory local government audit procedures are as follows. The end of year abstract of final accounts (current and capital) is sent by the local authority to the Department. The authority then receives an official Notice of Audit from the Department. Arrangements are next made for the carrying out of the audit, which means the authority gives public notice of the date of audit, notifies the audit to members and officials of the authority, and makes available books of accounts for public inspection prior to audit. Any interested persons may formally object to matters dealt with in the accounts and the objection must be considered by the auditor; the audit itself comprises detailed examination of the records of the authority and discussions with relevant officials. At the end of the audit, the auditor certifies the abstract of accounts, writes an audit report and draws the attention of the authority's management by means of a letter to specific issues not meriting mention in the report proper. The report is forwarded to the Minister, and finally the audit report is considered by the elected members at a meeting of the authority.

The local government audit is noteworthy in particular for the powers (often confused) of surcharge and charge. The Local Government (Ireland) Act, 1871 (section 12) empowers the auditor to surcharge any person who has made, or authorised the making of, an illegal payment. The Local Government (Ireland) Act, 1902 (section 20) allows the auditor to charge against any member or officer of the local authority the amount of any deficiency or loss incurred through their negligence or misconduct.[16] Instances of charges have always been rare, but surcharges were more common up to the mid-1970s. Nowadays the main importance of these powers lies in their residual value as deterrents.[17]

The local government audit is concerned mainly with financial regularity: the vouching of expenditure and receipts, verification of assets and liabilities, compliance with accounting policy and law, detection and prevention of error and fraud, rates of income collection. The focus is on whether all monies disbursed are properly authorised and accounted for and whether all monies receivable are collected and accounted for. In recent years, however, there has been an additional emphasis on 'value for money' in the public sector. It involves three concepts:-

- 'economy', mainly concerned with keeping the cost of 'inputs' (staff, materials, etc) at the lowest possible level consistent with a specified quantity and quality of service;
- 'efficiency', measuring the results of an organisation's activities as compared with the 'inputs' utilised. It is a ratio of 'inputs' to 'outputs' (e.g. the number of miles of new road built) or, preferably, to 'outcomes' (e.g. the actual economic and other benefits from new roads in terms of reductions in travel times and in injuries and deaths);
- 'effectiveness', a comparison between the specific objectives of an activity and the 'outcomes' achieved.[18]

Where a programme keeps costs to a minimum, produces good results from the resources it consumes and meets its objectives, it can be said to represent 'value for money'. In the local authority sector, the influence of such concepts can be seen in, for example, the increased use of cost-benefit analysis in the evaluation of major road projects, and in the establishment in 1993 by the Minister for the Environment of a Value For Money Unit within the local government audit service. Its purpose is to prepare reports analysing, and giving comparative data on, the cost of particular services across various local authorities so as to identify areas where improvements can be made. Reports have been completed on Purchasing, Advertising, Insurances, Parking Charges, Photocopying Costs, Machinery Yards and Energy Efficiency in Local Authority Buildings, and further reports are being prepared in relation to Differential Rents, Property Management, Public Lighting and Stores. Completed reports are issued to all local authorities and implementation is monitored at audit.[19]

The Local Government Act, 1991 (section 7) highlights the issue of value for money by requiring local authorities to have regard to certain matters in performing their functions. These matters include the available resources (from whatever source) and the need to secure the most beneficial, effective and efficient use of such resources; the need to maintain essential services and to achieve a reasonable balance between programmes; and the need for cooperation, coordination and consultation with other local authorities and public bodies as appropriate.

Central–Local Balance

In attempting to gauge the overall central-local balance, it is useful to maintain the distinction between the capital and current accounts. The overall level of local authority capital expenditure is determined within the framework of central government's PCP. In addition, there is supervision of individual programmes.

Policy in relation to capital expenditure on social housing is determined by central government, and implementation of policy is influenced by the Department of the Environment through a variety of means including: an annual allocation of housing 'starts' and capital funding to local authorities; the setting of standards for house construction and layout; the issuing of guidelines on issues such as the need to mitigate social segregation in housing and to promote inner city renewal; establishment of the terms and conditions of the various social housing schemes; and requirements to report to the Department on progress achieved. Reflecting this, national housing policy is often the subject of debate in Dáil Eireann and Seanad Eireann.[20]

Local authorities, however, retain a significant degree of

discretion in the detailed day-to-day administration of housing programmes. For example, the precise location of houses provided (either by new building or purchase) by local authorities, and the detailed needs to be catered for, are matters to be decided by the individual authorities within the programmes authorised by the Department. Similarly local authorities are free, in certain circumstances, to seek and accept tenders for housing construction schemes without prior Departmental approval.[21] The degree of discretion at local level in the implementation of housing policy generally has been subject to criticism on occasion, on the grounds of a perceived lack of national uniformity, and central government has also expressed concern on variations in local implementation of central government housing initiatives.[22]

Expenditure on improvement of national primary and secondary roads is subject to detailed control by the National Roads Authority, as it was formerly by the Department of the Environment. This reflects the clear view that national roads – as their title implies – are a national service most appropriately managed at central government level; it is also related to the level of EU funding for the programme and the consequent need to maximise benefits to Ireland from such funding.

Local authorities have more discretion in the case of non-national (i.e. regional, county and urban) roads, with central government providing a block grant for improvement works. Local authorities decide on the works to be undertaken with these funds, subject to conditions set by the Department. The situation is complicated, however, by the introduction in 1994 of a scheme of EU-aided central government grants under the Transport Operational Programme to meet the full cost of improvements to specific stretches of non-national road which will have a significant economic impact, by similar arrangements for INTERREG-funded schemes and by a new Exchequer-financed restoration programme which commenced in 1995. These schemes are subject to detailed supervision by the Department of the Environment, although in the case of the restoration programme primary discretion remains with county councils in relation to the selection of individual projects. [23]

The water supply and sewerage programme is also subject to Department supervision, with schemes requiring specific approval from the Custom House (actually O'Connell Bridge House) at each stage of the planning of a project. Less detailed supervision is applied in respect of the small schemes sub-programme.[24] Project-level controls also apply in relation to the smaller capital programmes: traffic management, urban and village renewal, fire and emergency services, libraries, swimming pools and waste recovery.

The conclusion, then, in relation to the capital account is that the balance is primarily, though not exclusively, weighted in favour of the centre. Given the nature of the services involved, the EU assistance available and the means of funding open to local authorities (an estimated 75 per cent of capital expenditure in 1995 was to be met by central government grants – see Table 3), this is not an unexpected outcome.

The situation on current account is more complex. The first thing to be said is that, unlike on capital account with its PCP allocations and programme-level supervision, central government does not seek to determine the level or composition of current expenditure. Local authorities are free to decide the level of current expenditure to be undertaken each year, and this decision is made by elected members as part of the annual process leading to adoption of estimates of expenses for the year. No quantitative limits are placed on local expenditure and no directions are given about the breakdown of planned expenditure between programmes. The Local Government (Financial Provisions) Act, 1978 (section 10(1)) gives the Minister for the Environment power, with the consent of the Minister for Finance, to limit amounts specified in estimates. This power, which was given to the Minister at a time of concern about possible demands on the Exchequer arising from the new domestic rate grant, has not been used and is unlikely to be.

The main influence of central government in relation to current expenditure lies in its role as provider of 36 per cent of local authority current income by way of grants – see Table 5. Firstly, in the case of the RSG, while there is no attempt to control local authority use of the grant, the amount of RSG (equivalent to 47 per cent of total current state grants to local authorities in 1995) is an important factor in determining the level of resources available to the local authority for a financial year and hence the expenditure plans of the authority. Secondly, other grants (for road maintenance, higher education, etc.) are not only limited in quantitative terms but are also, of course, earmarked for particular expenditure purposes even if within certain programmes (e.g. non-national roads) there is a measure of freedom as to how the funds are used.

An alternative to grant finance (albeit temporary) is borrowing. Under the Local Government (No. 2) Act, 1960, local authority borrowing is subject to the sanction of the appropriate Minister – usually the Minister for the Environment. Long-term borrowing is used to finance some limited capital expenditure as outlined in chapter 2. Short-term credit (usually in the form of overdraft) is necessary on both the current and capital accounts to meet gaps between the time when expenditure is incurred and the date of receipt of finance from grants, commercial/industrial rates, etc. Problems arise, however, if cyclical overdraft requirements become structural deficits on current account; they also occur if large debit balances need to be financed over a long period in respect of preliminary work on the planning of capital projects in advance of the schemes getting underway and grants becoming available. Review by the Department of local authority requests for sanction to overdraft, or other temporary forms of credit pending receipt of longer-term finance, aims to ensure that expenditure remains in line with local authority financial capacity.

Notwithstanding the role of central government in the provision of grants and its control of borrowing, the fact remains that if local authorities are free to determine the estimates of expenses, if 64 per cent of local authority current income comes from local sources over which they have some degree of control (e.g. commercial/industrial rates, housing rents, service charges) and if a large general grant is available in the form of RSG, local authorities retain a discretion as to the level of local expenditure and the purposes to which it will be applied. The discretion is there to be exercised even if each year there are inescapable ongoing commitments, as there are in most organisations, which limit the room for manoeuvre.

The Barrington Report

The Barrington Report considered the issue of central-local relations and recommended the following changes to underpin the role envisaged for local government as a partner in the overall system of government:

- Ireland should ratify the Council of Europe Charter of Local Self Government;
- there should be statutory recognition of local authorities as local democratic fora and of their general representational role;
- the next appropriate opportunity should be availed of to give constitutional recognition to local government.[25]

These changes would be in addition to a major programme of devolution of functions from the centre to local authorities.

Conclusion

The distinction between national and local services is one theoretical approach to central-local relations. Services can be regarded as national in character if, for example, they involve significant externalities or economies of scale, or if equity considerations point to uniformity in service standards or central government financing of relief from local taxes and charges. Local services are those from which efficiency gains can be realised by allowing expression to be given to varying local preferences for services; there are also political arguments for local decision-making. The concept of subsidiarity is often used by advocates of local determination and provision of services. National services may be financed by means of specific grants and local services by local taxes and/or general grants. In practice, it can be difficult to draw such clear distinctions between types of services.

There is a significant EU dimension to many local expenditure programmes; roads, water and sewerage services, urban and village renewal works, waste recovery facilities and other works benefit from Structural and Cohesion Funds. This dimension brings with it certain procedures for expenditure planning, evaluation and monitoring and requires EU priorities to be taken into account in determining sectors for investment. In general, local authorities have limited discretion in relation to the capital account where allocations are set, and individual programmes supervised, by central government; they have greater freedom over current account activities.

NOTES TO CHAPTER 3

1. D. Begg, R. Dornbusch and S. Fischer, *Economics*, London: McGraw Hill (1987), p. 340

2. Begg, Dornbusch and Fischer, *op. cit.*, p. 343

3. Ibid, p. 322

4. For an introduction to 'fiscal federalism' and for further references see J. Le Cacheux, 'Accountability Issues in Local Public Finance', in *The Financing of Local Government,* Dublin: Foundation for Fiscal Studies (1991)

5. The position in relation to subsidiarity is discussed in, C. Handy, *The Empty Raincoat: Making Sense of the Future,* Hutchinson (1994), pp. 115-28

6. *Government Statement on Local Government Reform,* 4 July 1995

7. *Commission Report to the European Council on the Adaptation of Community Legislation to the Subsidiarity Principle,* Brussels: Commission of the European Communities (1993)

8. R. O'Donnell, 'Regional Policy', in P. Keatinge (ed.), *Ireland and EC Membership Evaluated,* Dublin: IEA (1991), p. 63

9. *Ireland – National Development Plan 1994-1999,* Dublin: Stationery Office (1993), p. 14

10. *Ireland – National Development Plan 1989-1993*, Dublin: Stationery Office (1989), p. 10; *Ireland – National Development Plan 1994-1999*, Dublin: Stationery Office (1993), p. 14; *Ireland – Community Support Framework 1994-99,* Brussels: European Commission (1994), Table 2

11. Symposium of the Statistical and Social Inquiry Society of Ireland on 'The Use of Structural Funds', 4 March 1993

12. For these and subsequent road data, see *Operational Programme for Transport 1994-1999,* Dublin: Stationery Office (1994), p. 20

13. For further information on the Cohesion Fund see Council Regulation (EC) No. 1164 of 16 May 1994, published in *Official Journal of the European Communities,* 25 May 1994

14. For a general introduction to the Structural Funds see *EU Structural Funds: A Practical Guide*, Brussels: Irish Business Bureau (1995)

15. T.P. Golden, 'The Local Government Audit Service', in *Seirbhís Phoiblí,* Vol. 12, No. 1, April 1991, pp. 31-2

16. See R. Keane, *The Law of Local Government in the Republic of Ireland*, Dublin: The Incorporated Law Society of Ireland (1982), pp. 309-16, for an account of the law on surcharge and charge

17. Golden, *op. cit.,* p. 34

18. For an introduction to these concepts see P. Clarke, 'Performance Evaluation of Public Sector Programmes', *Administration,* Vol. 32, No. 3, Autumn 1984 and R. Boyle, 'Can Performance Monitoring in the Civil Service be as good as that in the Commercial Sector?', *Administration,* Vol. 37, No. 2, Summer 1989

19. *Official Report of Dail Debates*, 20 September 1995, Question No. 162

20. The latest statement of housing policy is *Social Housing – The Way Ahead*, Dublin: Department of the Environment (1995)

21. *Official Report of Dail Debates*, 7 March 1995, Question No. 85 and 20 June 1995, Question No. 135

22. National Economic and Social Forum, *Quality Delivery of Social Services*, Dublin: NESF (1995), paragraph 6.42; Department of the Environment, *op. cit.*, p. 37

23. Circular letters RW 1/94 of 4 February 1994 and RW 7/96 of 5 February 1996 from the Department to local authorities

24. For an account of water supply and sewerage programme procedures see *Operational Programme for Environmental Services 1994-1999,* Dublin: Stationery Office (1995), pp. 104-7

25. *Report of Advisory Expert Committee on Local Government*

Reorganisation and Reform, Dublin: Stationery Office (1991), p. 1. The Council of Europe Charter has been ratified by 19 European countries. The Minister for the Environment has indicated support for ratification of the Charter by Ireland – *Official Report of Dail Debates*, 27 April 1995, Question No. 7. The Local Government Act, 1991 (section 6) gave local authorities a general power to act to promote the interests of the local community

4
Principles of Local Taxation

Introduction

This chapter considers the case for local taxation. It also outlines criteria which may be used to evaluate a system of local taxation.[1] Principles which can be used to govern local taxation were set out by the Commission on Taxation in its Fourth Report, which considered the case for local taxation and the criteria which should be used to design an effective system, and by NESC, in its report on local authority finance.[2]

Why Local Taxation?

Since any system of local taxation involves variations in the rate of tax levied in different local authority areas, such a system is inevitably more complicated than a uniform national tax levied on the same base. Why then should the additional costs associated with a system of local taxation be incurred?

The additional costs arising from a system of local taxation are justified only if it is considered desirable as an objective of public policy to give local authorities full discretion to provide or not to provide local services. If they were given the power to provide such services but had no responsibility to raise the money to finance them, they would be under no pressure to weigh the costs and benefits of the services concerned. The corollary of allowing local authorities discretion in providing these services is to supply them with a tax base capable of financing the exercise of this discretion. There is no need to provide local authorities with an independent source of local finance if they are charged only with the local administration of national services, the level and nature of which are decided by central government.

Criteria to be Met

In designing a tax system it is important that the sum of the individual parts forms a coherent whole. Once the total system has been devised, parts of it can be allocated to different levels of government. In deciding which elements of the total tax system might be given to local authorities, the main considerations are:

- what is the required yield from local taxation?
- what taxes are the most suitable in this context?

Local taxes may be evaluated against the normal criteria of equity, efficiency and simplicity which are used to evaluate national tax systems, and against the criterion of accountability.

Equity

Equity is an essential quality of any tax system. Taxation in accordance with ability to pay provides an ideal to which almost everyone can subscribe. However, the ideal is difficult to achieve in practice. One can distinguish between the two dimensions of horizontal and vertical equity: persons in the same situation should be treated equally, and those more favourably situated should be required to pay more.

The notion underlying both aspects of equity implies that tax is a sacrifice levied on some kind of economic well-being. In practice, both the 'sacrifice' by way of tax and the 'well-being' on which the tax is levied have to be measured in money terms. Many of the most difficult questions in tax policy stem from the conventions that must be accepted when making the transition from the notion of economic well-being to the choice and exact definition of what is to be the measure of that – the tax base. In the context of local taxation, equity should take account of the impact of taxation and public expenditure at both national and local level, and should not be considered solely in relation to the individual local tax.

An alternative principle which might be considered as the basis for allocating taxation is that of 'benefit', which relates taxes to the benefits individuals are estimated to receive from goods and services provided by the State. Except in cases where revenue is raised in fees and charges for the direct use of publicly-provided services by particular individuals, this principle is difficult to apply.

Efficiency
Insofar as individuals when left to their own devices will spend their incomes wisely and business will choose the most efficient means of production, the minimisation of waste requires that a tax system should not influence individual or business choices. In general, this requirement of neutrality in a tax system means that taxation should not interfere with the relative rewards of the different types of work between which an individual may choose, the relative attractions of work and leisure, the relative returns from different types of investment decisions, or relative factor and goods prices. This concept of neutrality assumes that resources are being used in the most efficient manner before the imposition of the tax. This cannot always be taken for granted, because producers and consumers may fail to take account of externalities, therefore efficiency may be improved in some cases by a departure from neutrality. For this reason, tax concessions may aim at increasing the output of goods and services which it is desired to encourage. Alternatively, taxes may be imposed on activities which it is desired to discourage.

In the context of local taxation, an important aspect of efficiency is that local taxes can be levied at different rates in adjoining local areas without giving rise to serious distortions. It is essential that local authorities are able to set the rate of local taxation and, in particular, that adjoining local authorities can have different rates of taxation without causing intolerable distortions. However, this should not be carried too far. Even countries are constrained in their tax levels by the rates charged in neighbouring countries. For example, the excise duty on petrol in Ireland is limited by the rate charged in Northern Ireland. What is required is that some degree of variation is possible to allow different local authorities to choose different levels of taxation and spending in respect of local services.

Simplicity

It is desirable that the tax system is coherent, simple and straightforward. This means that the administrative costs of tax collection should be low and the compliance costs for the taxpayer in terms of money and mental effort should be small. Two aspects of simplicity should be noted in particular. When a complex operation is needed before liability can be ascertained, it is desirable that the taxpayer already needs to perform such operations for purposes unconnected with tax, for example keeping accounts. Secondly, the smaller the number of taxpayers for any given amount of revenue with whom the administration has to deal, the simpler is the system.

The criterion of simplicity imposes particular constraints in the area of local taxation. The fact that the county and county borough will remain the main units of local government in Ireland needs to be taken into account in evaluating a system of local taxation. It is not desirable to establish large and complex systems of tax administration at local level. However, in this context it is largely irrelevant whether local taxation is collected by the local authority or on an agency basis by the Revenue Commissioners (or some other body), provided the individual local authority has the discretion to vary the rate of tax levied in its own area.

It is also essential that there is a base for local taxes in each local authority area that is capable of yielding adequate revenue.

Accountability

It is important that the accountability of those who decide on taxes underpins every tax system, otherwise there is representation without taxation and/or taxation without representation. If there is no accountability, people may secure increases in public services without having to pay for them, and those without a voice in local affairs may have to meet the cost.

To promote accountability, it is desirable that if a local authority decides to increase or reduce the rate of local taxation the impact of such a change should bear on the local electorate. For this purpose it would be important that if central and local government share the same tax base, changes in the local rate of tax are not automatically fully offset by national changes as would be the case if local taxes were fully creditable against national taxes. The poll tax in the United Kingdom addressed the issue of accountability by providing that each individual on the electoral list was liable for the tax. However, as will be discussed in chapter 5, voting is not the only approach to the issue of accountability.

Conclusion

Local taxation policy must be seen in the context of national policy on taxation. In addition to the normal criteria of equity, efficiency and simplicity used to design national tax systems, attention should be given to the ability to have different rates of local taxes in adjoining areas without causing major distortions. This is important in Ireland given the small size of administrative units, a factor which also puts a premium on having local taxes that are simple to administer. Accountability is a further important criterion in the evaluation of local taxes. In practice, no local tax may meet fully all the criteria set out in this chapter, and policy-makers may have to make trade-offs between them in deciding how to proceed.

NOTES TO CHAPTER 4

1. The material in this chapter draws on 'Local Finance in Ireland – The Options' by D. de Buitleir – a paper presented to an IPA Conference, 'Rates and Property Valuation : The Challenge of the 1990s' on 12 September 1991 and published in Administration, Vol. 39 No. 4, Winter 1991

2. Commission on Taxation – Fourth Report, Special Taxation, Dublin: Stationery Office (1985); NESC, The Financing of Local Authorities, Dublin: NESC (1985)

5
VALUATION AND RATES

Introduction
Although the valuation and rating systems appear to be of little relevance to the study of present-day local government finance, owing to developments in recent decades, this is not in fact so. In the first place, rates on commercial/industrial property continue to be an important source of local authority finance. Furthermore, the distribution of RSG to local authorities was originally based on each authority's income from rates on domestic property and agricultural land at the time of the ending of such rates in 1978 and 1982 respectively, and is still a factor influencing the share-out. Finally, the experience with a local tax which provided a substantial portion of local government finance over a long period must be taken into account in the consideration of future financing options. This chapter, therefore, outlines the valuation and rating systems and describes how rates came to be limited to commercial/industrial property.

Valuation
The valuation and rating codes have been described by a High Court judge as 'a confusing mosaic of partly repealed and imperfectly drafted Victorian statutes encrusted with a century and a half's judicial decisions'.[1] The Valuation (Ireland) Act, 1852, the Valuation (Ireland) Amendment Act, 1854 and the Annual Revision of Rateable Property (Ireland) Amendment Act, 1860 are the core legislation governing valuation work. Two modern statutes, the Valuations Acts of 1986 and 1988, amended but did not fundamentally alter the law in this area. The system is operated by the Valuation Office, headed by the Commissioner of Valuation and under the aegis of the Minister for Finance.

The 1852 Act required that a valuation be carried out of all land and buildings in the country on the basis of their Net Annual Value. Land was to be valued by reference to the average price for the years 1849–51 of the main crops and produce of the time; the Net Annual Value of buildings was defined as their annual letting value over and above the cost of rates, repairs, insurance and maintenance. The valuation process required under the Act began in 1852 and was completed in 1865: it was known as 'Griffith's Valuation' after Sir Richard Griffith, under whose direction it was carried out.

'Griffith's Valuation' served for over a century as the basis for the levying and collecting of rates on land and buildings by local authorities, and is still the foundation for rates on commercial/industrial property. From the outset, however, there were doubts about the adequacy of valuations, especially land valuations. The valuation began in the South when the agricultural economy was depressed and was completed in Northern counties when conditions had improved; this left the latter valuations on average higher than the former. There was also concern at the quality of staff employed and the methods used.[2]

A further problem was that the law provided that the valuation of land could only be altered as part of a general revision of valuations in a local authority area. This could be instituted on the application by a local authority to the Minister for the Environment (in whom this power came to be vested) who could direct the Commissioner of Valuation to carry out the general revision. No such application was ever made by a county council and land valuations have remained generally unchanged since 1865.

The 1852 Act, however, provided for revisions of individual building valuations where circumstances served to alter the value of a property, and this process has been a continuous feature of the building valuation system. Following enactment of the Valuation Act, 1988, an owner or occupier of any property, the local authority or an officer of the Commissioner of Valuation can apply at any time for a revision of the valuation of any property. Applications are sent to the local authority who forward

them to the Commissioner; decisions on revision applications are
issued by the Commissioner early in February, May, August and
November of each year; not later than three days after their
receipt, local authorities must publish a notice indicating that
revision lists have been received and stating where they are
available for public inspection. There are two levels of appeal:

- an owner or occupier of property or the local authority can
  appeal the revision decision to the Commissioner, who must
  appoint an Appeal Valuer to deal with the case other than the
  one who made the original decision;
- an owner or occupier of property or the local authority can
  also appeal the Commissioner's appeal decision to a Valuation
  Tribunal from which appeals may be taken to the High
  Court on a point of law.[3]

While the law contains extensive provision for review of
individual building valuations, the position regarding the actual
determination of such valuations and the relationship between
them is not as clear-cut. As we have seen, the 1852 Act required
that the Net Annual Value of buildings should be determined by
reference to the annual letting value over and above the cost of
rates, repairs, insurance and maintenance. From the start, the
valuations used in the individual revisions process have been
lower than would be justified having strict regard to the then
current annual letting value. This practice, known as 'making
deductions to make relative' or 'maintaining the tone of the list',
was adopted in order to secure a degree of comparability between
the property being valued and similar properties in the locality
which were valued at an earlier date, and thereby to maintain
equity between ratepayers. It was given statutory backing by the
Valuation Act, 1986 (section 5).

However, the original intention behind the valuation code was
that regular general revisions of building valuations would secure
uniformity between them and that individual revisions would
merely maintain that uniformity until the next general revision.
The only general revisions carried out have been in the urban
areas of Dublin (1908-15), Waterford (1924-26), Galway (1946-

50) and Buncrana (1950) and these resulted in substantial increases in valuations. The question is whether, in the absence of general revisions as originally intended, the approach adopted through the years has been sufficient to ensure equity in the valuation of property still liable for rates. According to one practitioner, 'The real problem is the lack of a national revaluation as envisaged in the primary legislation'.[4]

Rates

Central government controls the major sources of tax revenue in Ireland (income and expenditure taxes) and their built-in revenue buoyancy; local government has direct access to one tax of significance. Rates are a local tax levied by county councils, county borough corporations, borough corporations and urban district councils on occupiers and, in the case of unoccupied property, owners of property valued for this purpose by the Commissioner of Valuation. However, where property is unoccupied, a refund is available for each month of vacancy provided the owner can demonstrate that repairs are being carried out or a tenant is being sought at a reasonable rent (Local Government Act 1946, sections 14 and 23, and separate statutes for the county borough corporations). The rate in the £ for each local authority is determined by it as part of the annual process of adopting estimates of expenses for the year; the liability of each ratepayer is determined by the multiplication of the rateable valuation of the property concerned by the relevant rate in the £ as determined by the local authority.[5]

The principal enactment governing the levying and collecting of rates is the Poor Relief (Ireland) Act, 1838. This Act established the poor rate, which was levied by Boards of Guardians for the purpose of administering poor relief in Ireland and came to be used by the new county councils established in Ireland in 1898. Other forms of rating in operation in the nineteenth century included grand jury cess and various municipal rates.

Today the two forms of rating in existence are the county rate and the municipal rate, which were established by sections 11 and 18 of the Local Government Act, 1946 and by separate legislation governing county borough corporations.[6] The existing 1838 law relating to the poor rate was adopted in the establishment of these two rates.

Rates had advantages as a source of local government finance. Using the criteria for local taxation outlined in chapter 4, they were a simple tax: administrative and compliance costs were low, the yield was predictable and substantial (though not buoyant) and the tax was difficult to evade. Rates also scored well on the accountability criterion: many of those who paid the tax could pass judgment at election time on those responsible for local expenditure and taxation decisions, or could otherwise influence such decisions. Furthermore, as real property could not be transferred from one local authority area to another, different local authorities could strike rates independently of each other without giving rise to serious distortions in trade; rates, therefore, satisfied the efficiency criterion and gave local authorities the power of local variation. Of course, if the power were abused by the levying of excessive amounts, it could happen that businesses would migrate from one area to another.

It was, however, the issue of equity which caused the major erosion of the rating system witnessed in recent decades. Before considering this matter, we will look briefly at other attenuations of the rating base.

Exemptions from Rates

From the commencement of the poor rate there were exemptions from rating, and these were added to in specific statutes over the years. The proviso to section 63 of the Poor Relief (Ireland) Act, 1838 gives the following exemptions from rating:

- turf banks when no rent or other valuable consideration is payable;
- mines for seven years after they are opened;
- churches, chapels or other buildings exclusively dedicated to religious worship or exclusively used for the education of the poor;
- burial grounds or cemeteries;

- infirmaries, hospitals, charity schools or other buildings used exclusively for charitable purposes;
- buildings, land etc. dedicated to or used for public purposes.[7]

Other statutory exemptions from rating include:

- premises used for the purposes of science, literature and the fine arts;
- certain plant and machinery[8];
- lighthouses, beacons and buoys;
- fisheries;
- oil wells for twenty years from the time oil is first extracted.

In addition, a local authority may remit two-thirds of rates due for ten years on premises provided for an industrial undertaking by, or with assistance from, (i) industrial development agencies in areas designated under the Industrial Development Act, 1986 or (ii) Údarás na Gaeltachta (the Údarás na Gaeltachta Act, 1979). Remissions are available for ten years on a sliding scale (full remission in year one; one-tenth remission in year ten) for new, enlarged or improved buildings in areas designated under the Urban Renewal Act, 1986; full remissions are available for ten years in respect of premises which are erected, enlarged or improved in the Temple Bar area of Dublin.[9] Finally, remissions were available for limited periods in respect of new, enlarged or improved premises up to 1976, and in respect of new or improved houses before the abolition of rates on domestic property.

In circumstances where exemptions from, or remissions of, local taxation serve national rather than local purposes, it has been argued that the cost should more appropriately be borne by central government rather than local taxpayers and that the terms of the reliefs should be set nationally.[10] This was, as we shall see, the practice in the case of further rate reliefs which applied to the agricultural sector.

End of Domestic Rates

The 1960s and early 1970s witnessed considerable discontent with rates. This was related to a rise in the burden which they represented due to the need to meet the cost of expanding services, including health services, roads and services to new housing areas which were developed at the time and which benefited from rate remissions. The amount payable in rates rose from £24 million in 1963-4 to £71 million in 1973-4, an increase of 105 per cent in real terms; the average rate in the £, a measure which discounts changes in the valuation base, rose from £2.33 in 1963-4 to £6.05 in 1973-4, an increase of 68 per cent in real terms.[11] While the burden of other forms of taxation was also rising, rates were a large and visible impost: they were payable in only two instalments until 1970, and their lack of buoyancy required regular increases in the rate in the £, increases which had to be adopted by the elected members of local authorities. In addition, rates were based on valuations which were increasingly questioned.

There was, however, more to it than that. Because rates were calculated by means of poundages applied to property values, rather than directly linked to ability to pay, the equity of the tax was increasingly subject to criticism. A number of studies of the subject lent some support to those opposed to rates as the system then operated. One concluded that 'rates are mildly regressive on most ranges of (household) income, but are sharply regressive in the lower income brackets'.[12] A more detailed study suggested that rates amounted to a constant proportion of income in the non-agricultural sector but might well be a regressive tax on owner-occupiers who were retired. The latter study went on to suggest changes in the rating system.[13] Criticism of rates on equity grounds was reinforced by the absence of formal schemes to waive the tax in hardship cases – the local authority merely had the power to declare rates irrecoverable after unsuccessful efforts had been made to secure payment.

Measures were taken to reform the system. The Local Government (Rates) Act, 1970 enabled rates to be paid in ten instalments if the ratepayer so wished; that Act also allowed local authorities to introduce schemes to waive rates in cases of hardship. In addition, the cost of public housing and health services was taken off the rates and made a charge on general taxation on a phased basis from 1973-4 up to 1977.

Reform did not, however, save the system. Fianna Fáil undertook in the course of the 1973 general election to de-rate houses and flats.[14] In the 1977 Budget, the Fine Gael/Labour Government which came to power in 1973 transferred the cost of one-quarter of domestic rates to central government, introducing a new domestic rate grant for this purpose, and hinted that they would shortly phase them out completely.[15] In the event, the new Fianna Fáil Government which took office that year enacted the Local Government (Financial Provisions) Act, 1978 which, with effect from 1 January 1978, terminated rates liability on domestic dwellings, secondary schools, community halls and farm buildings not previously exempt from rates.

The 1978 Act (section 9) provided formally for a central government grant to meet the cost of domestic rates income foregone by local authorities. However, to control the Exchequer's liability, the Minister for the Environment was empowered, with the consent of the Minister for Finance, to place a limit on the percentage increases in rate poundages determined annually by local authorities (section 10(2)); this power was exercised between 1978-82 inclusive. The Local Government (Financial Provisions) (No.2) Act, 1983 (section 9) modified the link between the cost of domestic rates income foregone and the level of grant received: in future, the grant need only not exceed (and could, therefore, be less than) the amount required to meet in full the cost of derating domestic property. The Minister retained the legal power to limit increases in rate poundages but in practice, since then, local authorities have been free to determine these. (The 1983 Act also widened local charging powers.) The Local Government Act, 1994 (sections 47 and 48) finally ended the formal legal obligation on local authorities to apply rates in the £ to domestic valuations and removed any link between the grant and domestic rate reliefs; it provides for the application of the rate in the £ to commercial/industrial valuations only and for the payment of a grant each year to rating authorities.

End of Rates on Land

An Agricultural Grant payable to local authorities was introduced in 1898 to alleviate the burden of rates on land. It enabled local authorities to extend what came to be progressively more significant rate reliefs to the agricultural sector. The scheme of reliefs for 1982 provided for:

- 100 per cent relief for holdings with land valuations of less than £50;
- 75 per cent relief for holdings of £50 and over, but less than £70;
- 50 per cent relief for holdings of £70 and over.

There was also an undertaking by the Government to fully relieve rates on land from 1983 onwards.[16]

These reliefs and the prospect of more to come did not, however, make the land rating system immune to challenge. The High Court concluded in July 1982, in a case taken by a number of Wexford farmers (*Brennan and others* vs *The Attorney General*), that the valuation system was inconsistent with the Constitution. The Supreme Court, in a judgment of similar effect but in different terms, decided on appeal in January 1984 that reasonable uniformity in valuation was essential in the interests of equitable taxation, that the 1852-65 land valuation did not provide such uniformity and that individual ratepayers had no means of redress against inequity. Accordingly, section 11 of the Local Government Act, 1946, insofar as it permitted the levying of rates on land, was found to be unconstitutional.

The immediate effect of the July 1982 judgment was that rates on land were no longer collectable. The Agricultural Grant became a grant to local authorities to compensate them for income which they would otherwise have received from, or in respect of, rates on land. In 1988 it was merged with the domestic rate grant and the bounty in lieu of rates on Irish and foreign government property, which was paid by the Exchequer to local authorities, to form a single RSG.[17] These events also opened the way for farmers to be fully integrated into the income tax system – up to then only farmers with holdings above certain land valuations were liable to income tax. Before this finally happened, however, there was a short interlude.

A new farm tax was announced as part of the Government's

National Plan, *Building On Reality, 1985-1987*, on 2 October 1984. The tax was designed to double the yield from farmer taxation by 1986. To this end, the Government proposed that farmers be treated for tax purposes as follows:

(i) those with under twenty adjusted acres	: liable for neither farm tax nor income tax
(ii) those with at least twenty but less than eighty adjusted acres	: liable for farm tax only
(iii) those with eighty adjusted acres or over	: liable for income tax and farm tax, with the latter allowed as a credit against the former.

The process of classifying land according to adjusted acreage (i.e. its potential productivity) began in September 1985. The progress which had been made by September 1986 allowed the tax to be first applied to farms of 150 adjusted acres and over, at a rate of £10 per adjusted acre. The sum of £5.2 million was levied by local authorities, beginning in November 1986, on over 2,100 holdings in respect of farm tax due for 1986; £4.3 million was collected. The new Fianna Fáil minority Government, which took office in March 1987, announced the abolition of farm tax.

The farm tax had the advantage of simplicity. However, as the tax level was set by central government, it did not promote accountability and there was no power of local variation. The tax would also have done little to secure more efficient agricultural production. Finally, as the tax was based on potential productivity it would have given rise to serious inequity between taxpayers.[18]

Rates on Commercial/Industrial Property

Rates remain today only on commercial/industrial property. Local authority income from this source amounted to an estimated £323 million in 1995.[19]

Apart from the issue of the valuation system which was referred to earlier, the question has also arisen of the merits of this tax in terms of accountability. The matter was addressed by United Kingdom-based consultants for NESC in 1985. Their conclusion was: 'As presently arranged, this tax fails the basic test of accountability'.[20] The argument was related to the fact that businesses have no votes at local elections and that the cost of commercial/industrial rates may ultimately be borne by people living outside the local authority area (customers, shareholders, workers); hence, businesses could be 'exploited' for the benefit of those who live in the area and are entitled to vote, although it was admitted that this had not in fact occurred. This concern appears to be supported by the fact that the total amount due in commercial/industrial rates has been rising in real terms.

It can also be argued, however, that as rates are allowable as an expense in the calculation of income and corporation tax liabilities, the net amount due is less than appears at first sight. Furthermore, the benefits to business from local authority activities, as well as the costs, need to be taken into account. Finally, although business does not have a vote, it is not without a say in the determination of the local rate in the £. As would be expected, business interest groups seek to influence the level of local taxation they have to bear, and local authority members (some of whom would be local businessmen) and officials are conscious of the possible adverse effects of their decisions on the local economy, particularly in the context of decisions on rates by neighbouring authorities. Accordingly, accountability is not only a matter of voting.

The problems of accountability which arose in the United Kingdom and which appear to have prompted the above criticism were related to the actions of left-wing local councils. These councils were elected mainly by lower income groups, who benefited from rate rebates, and were perceived as having determined levels of public services without sufficient regard for those who ultimately had to pay for them through local taxes; they had a particular incentive to do this as local authorities in the United Kingdom have a significant role in the provision of social services. This particular combination of conditions does not necessarily obtain in Ireland.

Conclusion

The valuation system has its origins in the middle of the last century. Problems with the equity of the tax contributed significantly to the ending of rates on domestic property in 1978 and on agricultural land in 1982. Apart from derating of these sectors, there are substantial exemptions from, and remissions of, rates, the cost of which is borne by local taxpayers. Rates, long the mainstay of local government finance, are now paid by the commercial/industrial sector only and yielded an estimated £323 million in 1995. Differing views have been expressed on the question of accountability in the context of the operation of commercial/industrial rates.

NOTES TO CHAPTER 5

1. Mr. Justice Costello reported in *The Irish Times*, 11 May 1989, giving judgment in a case concerning the valuation of a chemical plant in Cork
2. D. de Buitleir, *Problems of Irish Local Finance*, Dublin: IPA (1974), p. 11
3. This part draws on T. O'Connor, 'Valuation Office', *Seirbhís Phoiblí*, Vol. 12, No. 1 (April 1991), pp. 4-14
4. S. Rogers, Commissioner of Valuation, quoted in *The Irish Times*, 12 March 1991. General revision of valuations has been recommended in many reports. For example, see *Report of Advisory Expert Committee on Local Government Reorganisation and Reform*, Dublin: Stationery Office (1991), p. 39
5. The procedures involved are set out in D. Roche, *Local Government in Ireland*, Dublin: IPA (1982), pp. 168-9
6. Section 63 of the Local Government (Dublin) Act, 1930; section 25 of the Limerick City (Management) Act, 1934; section 24 of the Waterford City Management Act, 1939; section 16 of the Cork City Management (Amendment) Act, 1941; and section 5 of the Local Government (Reorganisation) Act, 1985 for Galway

7. For a discussion of these exemptions see R. Keane, *The Law of Local Government in the Republic of Ireland*, Dublin: The Incorporated Law Society of Ireland (1982), pp. 289-99

8. This exemption has been the subject of considerable controversy. See O'Connor, *op. cit.,* pp. 10-11

9. Urban Renewal Act, 1986 (Remission of Rates) Scheme 1995 and Urban Renewal Act, 1986 (Remission of Rates) (No.2) Scheme 1995 – S.I. Nos. 364 and 365 of 1995

10. For example, see J. Copeland and B. Walsh, *Economic Aspects of Local Authority Expenditure and Taxation*, Dublin: ESRI (1975), p. 110

11. Department of the Environment, *Returns of Local Taxation 1963-4* and *1973-4*, Dublin: Stationery Office; *CSO Statistical Bulletin*, March 1994

12. De Buitleir, *op. cit.,* p. 29

13. J. Copeland and B. Walsh, *op. cit.,* p. 18

14. D. Roche, *Local Government in Ireland*, Dublin: IPA (1982), p. 156

15. *Official Report of Dáil Debates*, volume 196, columns 275-278, 26 January 1977

16. Circular letter Fin. 11/82 of 4 May 1982, from the Department of the Environment to local authorities

17. RSG now also includes former specific grants to local authorities to compensate them for the exemption of private fisheries from rates, and a grant to meet 50 per cent of the cost of preparing and maintaining the electoral register

18. For elaboration of these arguments see M. Coughlan, *The Farm Tax*, unpublished M.Sc. (Econ.) dissertation submitted to Trinity College Dublin and the Institute of Public Administration, 1991, and 'Farm Tax Policy-Making', *Administration*, Vol. 42, No. 2, Summer 1994

19. Department of the Environment, *Local Authority Estimates 1995*, Dublin: Stationery Office (1995)

20. NESC, *The Financing of Local Authorities*, Dublin: NESC (1985), p. 39

6
LOCAL TAXATION OPTIONS

Introduction

This chapter looks at options for increasing the share of local taxation in the overall financing of local authorities, if this is desired as a policy objective.[1] There are a number of options, which are not mutually exclusive and could form part of a package of local taxes. As shown in chapter 2, only in relatively few countries are local authorities confined to a single tax.

Equity

As was noted in chapter 4, equity is a most important criterion against which to evaluate taxes. However, it is less important than assessing the overall acceptability of the tax and public expenditure systems. It is not a matter of great importance if an individual tax, considered in isolation, is unfair, if this is offset by other elements of taxation and public expenditure. For example, the excise duty on tobacco is regressive but this is regarded as acceptable because of the progressive character of other public policies. For this reason, in the following discussion, there is no major focus on the equity aspects of particular local tax options.

Local Motor Tax

At present owners of motor vehicles are required to pay motor tax to the local authority in whose area the vehicle is ordinarily kept. Owners of fleets of vehicles (i.e. 6 vehicles or over) have the option of taxing the vehicles where the head office of the company is located. Local authorities remit the proceeds to central government.

It seems administratively feasible that motor tax could be transferred to local authorities who would have the power to change the rate of tax. The tax could be levied on the basis of the residence of the owner. It would be possible for fleet operators to register their vehicles in local authority areas with lower rates of tax. However, this would not unduly inhibit the possibility of local variation in the rate of tax. The tax is relatively simple to administer and there would be no great distortion of economic activity.

The yield from motor tax in 1995 is estimated to be £241 million so the tax provides scope for allocating to local authorities a significant revenue source. It may also be that collection and enforcement of the tax would be improved if the revenue accrued locally. However, different car ownership rates between local authority areas could present difficulties in ensuring that each local authority had an adequate tax base.

As regards the criterion of accountability, the tax base would be relatively wide. While motor vehicle ownership rates are not as high as in some other countries, the impact of these taxes is borne directly by a significant part of the electorate.

Local Property Tax

It has been argued that the Irish system of taxation is defective due to the relatively low taxation of owner-occupied residential property, notwithstanding the existence of the residential property tax controlled by the central government.[2] The imposition of such a tax could allow substantial reductions in the rates of other taxes, which could be used to make the level of these taxes competitive with those applying in the EU.[3] Such a tax could be imposed at either local or national level, but does offer the possibility of providing independent local revenue.

Property tax is suitable as a local tax as the location of property is fixed and wide differences in the levels of tax would not cause undue distortions. The tax scores particularly well on the criterion of local variation. The tax could be collected either at local or national level; all that is necessary is that local authorities determine the rate. It may, however, be argued that local authorities should administer and collect any local property tax as they would have the incentive to do so properly. The Commission on Taxation in 1985 concluded that a tax on residential and other property (excluding land) is the most suitable form of local taxation; NESC came to a similar conclusion in their study that year but disagreed on the question of the treatment of land under any such tax.

Callan has set out the principles and policy options that are available in the area of property tax.[4] Briefly, four options are considered. These are:

- the inclusion of imputed income from owner-occupation in the income tax base;
- a simpler property tax at a flat percentage rate on all owner-occupied property, without any rebates for those on low incomes;
- a property tax which would apply only to properties valued above a certain limit, and applying only to the excess of property value above that limit;
- a property tax with an exemption for those on the lowest incomes, and a reduced liability ('marginal relief') for those on incomes slightly above the cut-off point.

In general, a local property tax could follow the principles embodied in the residential property tax and be levied on the self-assessed market values of owner-occupied houses. A waiver scheme would be required to cater for hardship cases in order to improve the equity of the property tax.

Local Income Tax

Local income tax is a possibility as a candidate for local taxation; it is possible to levy significantly different rates of tax on people living in adjoining areas, as the experience along the border with Northern Ireland shows. However, there are a number of problems to be overcome before local income tax could be considered. The existing marginal tax rate of a single person on average earnings is 56 per cent, so there could be efficiency losses if rates were increased, and local authorities could be very constrained in raising tax rates.[5]

Bearing in mind the administrative complexities, it appears that the only realistic basis on which a local income tax could be contemplated in Ireland is for it to be administered on an agency basis by the Revenue Commissioners, with each local authority determining the rate. This means that the base for local income tax would have to be the same as for national income tax. The Revenue Commissioners would then pass on the appropriate amounts to the different local authorities.

One possibility is a local addition to each of the national rates of tax expressed as pence in the pound – the pence method. Special combined tax tables to collect national and local tax would have to be provided to employers for each rate of local tax. These would require revision whenever local or national tax rates changed.

At present there are four national PAYE tables. If there were ten different rates of local tax the present system would require forty tax tables. While there would be no additional calculations for employers, the selection of the appropriate tax tables would give rise to errors. In practice, small employers might not have to deal with much more than the existing four tables if all their employees lived in the same local authority area. Larger employers with computerised payroll operations could be expected to cope better with the additional work involved.

A more progressive form of local income tax would be a local addition (surcharge) of a percentage to each individual's national tax bill. The local rate of tax would be expressed as a percentage of a national tax. The amount of national/local income tax due in each pay period could be determined by reference to a ready reckoner or conversion table. The employer would have to calculate the national taxes as now and apply the percentage addition. This would mean an additional calculation. Both forms of local income tax would allow flexibility between local authorities and in the total sums raised, but the surcharge method would make the local tax yield very sensitive to changes in the national tax yield.

A number of other problems would have to be overcome before local income tax could be introduced. These relate to determination of taxpayer's residence, treatment of investment income and treatment of company profits. While these are difficulties, local income tax is levied in twelve of the sixteen countries discussed in chapter 2.

It would be necessary to determine the taxpayer's principal place of residence for local tax purposes. Under the present system the Revenue Commissioners do not necessarily know or need to know the location of residence. PAYE taxpayers have most of their dealings with employers. The taxpayer's address, which may be held incidentally on the Revenue Commissioners' files, would not be conclusive evidence for deciding which local rate of tax should be applied. For self-employed taxpayers, the Revenue Commissioners have on record the taxpayer's business address, which may be in a different local authority area from his residence. To deal with this problem, taxpayers would have to disclose the local authority area in which they resided. A procedure would have to be established for determining each year the taxpayer's place of residence for local tax purposes.

The most practicable scheme would be to set liability each year for the appropriate local rate of tax on the basis of residence at a particular date prior to the tax year. In principle, residence should be established as near as possible to the start of the tax year to ensure that it is as up-to-date as possible. Changes in residence after the date of residence determination would only have effect for future years. For most taxpayers, determination of residence would be fairly easy; for others, including members of the defence forces and others with no permanent homes, special provisions would be necessary. It would take time to record the residence of every income tax payer in the State, but it would be feasible if the necessary resources were devoted to it.

The taxation of investment income (including capital gains) at different local rates would be difficult for some types of investment income. Where tax is deducted at source, such as by banks and building societies on deposit interest, it would be difficult for such institutions to apply the correct local tax rate. Special arrangements would be necessary for the taxation of certain deposit interest which has been reduced to 15 per cent because of the constraints imposed by the low rates imposed in other countries in an environment in which there are no exchange controls. A means of dealing with investment income generally might be for self-employed taxpayers to deal with it under the normal self-assessment procedures and for it to be dealt with on review of PAYE cases.

Should a local income tax apply to company profits? If the answer is yes, the only practicable means of doing so is to levy the local tax rate applicable in the area in which the company has its registered office, with the result that areas such as Dublin City would benefit enormously. A local income tax applying to company profits would mean that the benefit of the 10 per cent rate of tax on manufacturing would be eroded. An alternative is to apply the rate of local tax to distributed profits only – presumably exempting charities and pension funds. Another option is to retain rates on commercial/industrial property in lieu of a local tax charge on company profits. Whatever solution is adopted, the local taxation of company profits would create distortions and anomalies of some kind.

Local VAT

Local sales taxes have obvious attractions since most shopping is done within the local authority area in which people live; they also provide a means of charging tourists for the use of local amenities. However, the extent to which variation in local sales taxes gives rise to changes in shopping patterns would reduce the efficiency of such instruments as local taxes.

The administrative feasibility of operating a national value-added tax and separate local authority supplements is open to question. The present national structure of VAT has five rates: zero; a special rate of 2.5 per cent on livestock; reduced rates of 10 and 12.5 per cent; and a standard rate of 21 per cent. To avoid complications, it would be desirable that local authorities adopt the same structure, with a local addition to one or all of these national rates. A problem with local VAT is that local and national VAT paid in one area would have to be allowed as a credit against local and national VAT paid in another area, and refunds given in appropriate cases. It would, therefore, present problems of accountability in so far as local authorities could increase their revenue from local VAT at the expense of the Exchequer and possibly other local authorities.

Let us assume that all the beer consumed in Tipperary is manufactured in Dublin. The beer is valued at £1000 and half the value added is generated in Dublin and half in Tipperary. The national rate of VAT is 10 per cent and the local VAT rate is 5 per cent in each area. The VAT revenue on beer consumed in Tipperary is £150, that is £1000 at 15 per cent. This is divided as follows: £100 to the Exchequer, £25 each to local authorities in Dublin and Tipperary.

Look what happens if Dublin decides to increase its VAT rate to 10 per cent, taking its revenue to £50. This £50 under the VAT system is allowed as a credit against liability at the next stage. Because the rate of VAT in Tipperary remains unchanged, consumers of beer in Tipperary continue to pay VAT of £150. There are two alternatives. If local and national VAT are linked the extra credit is divided equally between the national Exchequer and Tipperary local authorities and their yield is Exchequer £80 and Tipperary £20. Alternatively, local VAT might be creditable only against local VAT, and the result would be that Tipperary would have to refund a total of £25 while the Exchequer would retain £100. In either event, the effect would be to have a system which would be flawed and which would have the disadvantage of taxpayers being unclear about where the money was going.

The only alternative is to have some central adjustment to offset this. This would be complicated. Indeed attempts to move to a destination system of VAT at EU level and so avoid border adjustments have so far failed, due to the complexity and unreliability of the central adjustment system.

Local Green Taxes

There is a growing international trend towards the introduction of green taxes to penalise environmentally-damaging activity.[6]

The following advantages have been put forward for using charges and taxes as a means of environmental management:

- it is more efficient because it encourages polluters who can reduce emissions cheaply to take advantage of this fact, while accepting that very high clean-up costs will face those who pollute relatively more. More environmental improvement per pound spent results from this method than from a standard approach which requires each polluter to meet a particular emission standard;

- it allows the producer to decide how emissions are to be reduced. This might be through a change in input mix, a process change, treatment of some emissions or some combination of these. The regulatory approach tends to emphasise 'end of the pipe' technology i.e. treatment of emissions;

- it puts constant pressure on the polluter to do better. Under the regulatory approach, once the standard is met there is no incentive to improve;

- it generates funds which can – but of course need not – be used for overall environmental management, including the provision and operation of collective treatment facilities.

Charging for pollution is most appropriate where there are relatively few polluters and the pollution is emitted from readily identifiable sources. Where these conditions do not apply, it is difficult to implement an effective scheme. Taxes on effluent are not appropriate in all cases. However, they are appropriate in cases in which there is a relatively small number of sources of pollution which can be monitored without undue cost. Some of the most difficult environmental management cases arise where there are a large number of polluters. In such instances, both taxes/charges and regulations have severe limitations.

It is difficult to see pollution charges becoming a source of substantial local authority income. Indeed, it would be unacceptable if they were as it would imply a high level of pollution. However, local taxes on activities which cause pollution have a role to play in protecting the environment. Existing control provisions under the Local Government (Water Pollution) Acts, 1977-90 allow charges to be prescribed for discharges to waters and for contributions to be levied towards the costs incurred by local authorities in connection with discharges to sewers. Under the Derelict Sites Act, 1990, local authorities charge a levy on derelict urban land.

Conclusion

This chapter has outlined options for local taxes. It discusses motor, property, income, sales and green taxes as options to give local authorities increased powers of local taxation to finance the provision of local services, if this is a desired objective of public policy.

NOTES TO CHAPTER 6

1. The material in this chapter draws on The Fourth Report of the Commission on Taxation, *Special Taxation*, Dublin: Stationery Office (1985). The ground is also covered in D. de Buitleir, 'Local Finance in Ireland – The Options', in *Administration*, Vol. 39, No. 4, Winter 1991

2. 'Given the pressures on revenue, the Council considers that further reductions in taxes on earned income are only possible with measures to broaden the tax base including the introduction of a comprehensive property tax.' NESC, *A Strategy for the Nineties*, Dublin: NESC (1989)

3. For a discussion of the possible role of Irish property taxation in the context of the pressures on the Irish tax base arising from the EU Single Market, see D. de Buitleir and D. Thornhill, *EMU and Irish Fiscal Policy*, Dublin: Institute of European Affairs, (1993), pp. 55-7

4. T. Callan, *Property Tax : Principles and Policy Options*, ESRI Policy Research Series, Paper No. 12, July 1991

5. OECD, *Economic Survey, Ireland 1995*, Paris, OECD (1995), p. 46

6. For a discussion of taxation and the environment see *Tax Policy in OECD Countries*, Amsterdam: Ken Messere IBFD Publications (1993), chapter 7E. See comments on the issue as it affects Ireland in Department of Finance, *Financial Statement of the Minister for Finance 1996*

7
CENTRAL GOVERNMENT GRANTS

Introduction
This chapter examines the role of central government grants in local finance. It details the principal reasons for such grants, the various types of grants are discussed and the typology is applied to the Irish grant system. Finally, some specific issues are discussed relating to the system as it currently operates.

Justification
It is evident from Table 7 that central government grants play a significant role in the financing of sub-national governments in developed countries. While the purposes served by grants depend in any particular case on the overall local financial system, at a theoretical level we can postulate at least four reasons for such a role:

- the local finance system can be based on grants rather than on local taxation. It is entirely feasible, though not without implications for the extent of local discretion (overall expenditure levels being determined by central government), to finance local government in full by means of central government grants and, as Table 7 shows, Italy and the Netherlands come close to doing this; [1]
- where local taxation contributes to local finance, it is unlikely to be sufficient to provide local government on the required scale and, in such circumstances, local taxes need to be supplemented by grants;
- it may be considered unreasonable to expect the cost of the provision of national services to be met out of local taxation so central government may, for example, provide grants to

finance the externality involved, to capture economies of scale, to secure designated service standards or to provide relief of local taxation to certain categories of local taxpayers;

- it may also be felt unreasonable to expect local taxpayers to pay significantly different amounts from one local authority area to another solely because spending needs or taxable resources vary by appreciable amounts. Accordingly, grants could be paid with the aim of promoting equalisation as between local taxpayers in different areas.

Grant Typology

Figure 3 sets out a typology of central government grants.[2] General (or lump-sum) grants are used at the discretion of the local authority; specific grants are earmarked for certain expenditure programmes or projects.

General grants can be distributed at the discretion of central government or may in some way be required to be disbursed according to what are considered to be objective measures of expenditure need and/or taxable capacity/local tax effort.

Non-matching specific grants are allocated to local authorities at the discretion of central government and do not require local fiscal effort. Matching specific grants require such an effort and are based either on costs to the local authority or on the authority's performance in the production of an output. Cost-based specific grants may be open-ended, proportional to any level of local expenditure, or closed-ended, not subsidising ex penditure beyond a certain upper cash limit.

General grants have an income effect, increasing the total resources available to the local authority. They stimulate expenditure according to the income elasticity of demand for services and do not alter the incentives facing the authority; they are commonly availed of where central government wishes to use grants in lieu of, or to supplement, local taxation or to promote equalisation between local authorities. Specific grants, operating through relative price (or substitution) effects, reduce the price of a service from the local authority's point of view and lead to an increase in production of the service in accordance with its price

Figure 3: Central Government Grants

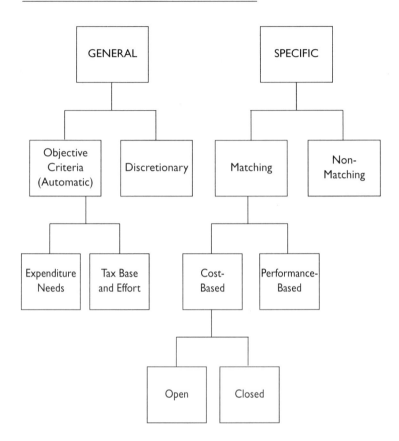

elasticity. They are best suited to circumstances where it is desired to secure the provision of a national service which otherwise would not receive the same priority at local level.

Grant System in Ireland

The Irish grant system includes the general RSG, whose origins lie in a need to replace a form of local taxation with another source of income, thereby allowing local government to provide the same level of service to the community. In addition, there are many specific grants aimed at assisting the provision of services in the different local authority areas. The extent to which the grant system takes into account, or should take into account, equalisation between such areas has been the subject of some discussion in recent years. This matter is dealt with further below.

Table 9 applies the grant typology outlined above to the main grants in Ireland. It can be said that:

- general grants (i.e. RSG) comprised an estimated 47 per cent of current grants and 19 per cent of total grants to local authorities in 1995;

Table 9: Typology of Central Government Grants in Ireland

Type	Grant	Comment
General	RSG	Distributed broadly in proportion to rates income foregone following ending of domestic and agricultural rates
Specific Non-Matching	Higher Education	
	National Road Management and Maintenance	
	Block Grants for Improvement/Maintenance of Non-National Roads★ Non-National Road Restoration★ (Improvement and Maintenance) VEC Superannuation	
	Motor Tax Collection, Driver Licensing, Vehicle Testing	
	Social Housing Capital Works	Although Table 3 indicates non-Exchequer sources of

Type	Grant	Comment
		funding, ultimately housing capital costs are almost all met in full by way of central government grants/subsidies
	National Road Improvement	
	Non-National Road Improvement (EU-aided)	
	Water and Sewerage Services Capital Works Fire and Emergency Services Capital Works	Excluding small schemes (see below)
	Library Capital Works	
	Renovations to Swimming Pools	
Specific Matching	New Swimming Pools	Closed-Ended
	Urban and Village Renewal Capital Works	Closed-Ended
	Dublin Traffic Management	Closed-Ended
	Small Water and Sewerage Services Capital Works	Closed-Ended
	Community Employment	Closed-Ended
	Waste Recovery	Closed-Ended

*These grants are regarded at central government level as a supplement to, not a substitute for, local authority own resources expenditure on non-national roads – e.g. see Department of the Environment Press Releases of 18 February 1994, 26 July 1995 and 5 February 1996 in which Ministers emphasised the need for local authorities to maintain their own financial commitment to such roads. As such, these grants contain matching elements. In addition, local authorities have discretion as to which specific stretches of road benefit from the grants.

- specific grants made up 53 per cent of current grants and 81 per cent of total grants in 1995;
- all capital grants were specific;
- most specific grants were non-matching and were project-specific, rather than being devoted to categories of expenditure with local authorities free to determine the particular benefiting projects.

There is no significant central government funding for management and maintenance of local authority housing and of water and sewerage facilities, services which are often regarded as being 'national' in character. There is, however, evidence of increased central government concern in these areas: for example a grant scheme, along with other measures, was announced in 1995 for pilot projects in the management of local authority housing and this followed earlier related initiatives. Under the Housing Management Grant Scheme the Department recoups 50 per cent of expenditure incurred by local authorities on approved projects, subject to a limit of £10,000. The sum of £100,000 was made available for the scheme in 1995.[3]

Equalisation

Financial equalisation may be defined as the achievement of an equitable, or a more equitable, distribution of financial resources between sub-national governmental authorities. If central government has an overall concern with the range and quality of public services, and if local authorities have varying financial capacity, it follows that if it is not to resort to centralised provision of all services, central government may wish to take measures to assist those local authorities with relatively high expenditure needs or a low taxable capacity. A similar argument applies, and is advanced by Ireland, to the relations between the EU and less prosperous member states.

General grants are the most commonly used means of financial equalisation although in certain circumstances, related to the criteria for allocation of the grants and the rate of assistance, specific grants may also contribute to this end. A further, more economically efficient, option would be horizontal transfers from 'well-off' to 'less well-off' local authorities, but this could be expected to face significant difficulties in gaining acceptance from the various interests concerned. Equalisation systems typically seek to compensate for disparities in expenditure needs as measured by appropriate indicators and/or to equalise, or at least approximate, *per capita* revenue at uniform tax rates given the local taxation base.

An issue in local government finance in recent years has been whether RSG is distributed in an equitable manner between local authorities and, if not, the changes to present arrangements which might be made towards this end. The distribution of RSG still broadly reflects the level of income foregone by local authorities as a result of the abolition of domestic rates and the ending of rates on land; that is, the proportion received by each authority has its origins in the authority's proportion of the total income from domestic and agricultural rates in 1977.[4] This situation has arisen due to the circumstances of the attenuation of the rating system, the use of uniform rate increases in 1978-82 and the subsequent application of any change in the global RSG total, determined annually by central government, on a uniform basis amongst local authorities. RSG, therefore, does not expressly take into account differences in expenditure needs and taxable resources at local level: its primary purpose was to replace lost income.

It has been argued that the problem should not be exaggerated, at least as far as it concerns the early years of operation of the present system. The proportionate distribution between local authorities depends on the rate in the £ levied by each authority at its own discretion, and the rateable valuation, in 1977; the rate in the pound could be taken as a fair measure of spending need, and *per capita* rateable valuations were fairly even across the country.[5] The relevance of such arguments was likely to diminish over time, as the comparative spending needs of local authorities changed and authorities with a large commercial/industrial valuation base were able to avail of their greater revenue-raising powers. And while the extensive use of specific non-matching grants may have played a role in promoting equalisation (e.g. directing capital funds to areas of greatest need; using varying rates of central government subsidy for water and sewerage schemes prior to the introduction of 100 per cent grants in 1988; reflecting these varying rates of subsidy in RSG adjustments in that year), demands grew for more transparent measures to address the issue.

The 1991 Advisory Expert Committee on Local Government Reorganisation and Reform had, as one of its terms of reference, 'to make recommendations on the criteria on which the contribution from central funds to local authorities should be made on a statutory basis'.[6] The resulting Barrington Report recommended that the following principles should underpin the distribution of central funds to local authorities:

1. As far as possible central government grants should be consolidated into a single general equalisation grant which should be distributed to local authorities in a manner which takes account of needs and resources.

2. Maximum discretion should be given to local authorities insofar as local spending priorities are concerned.

3. Local authorities should have a meaningful input into the annual budgetary process which determines the amount of central funding which will be available for distribution to local authorities.

4. The distribution of central funds to local authorities should be capable of adjustment to take account of future devolution of functions.

5. Specific purpose grants should, insofar as practicable, be confined to situations where the benefits flowing from the expenditure accrue substantially to people outside the area of the local authority.

6. As there can be no increase in overall public expenditure, the introduction of an equalisation system is likely to result in gainers and losers in local authorities as funding comes more to reflect actual needs and resources. The transition to such a system would have to be phased in over a period of years.[7]

A related report prepared by the Institute for Fiscal Studies found the Irish specific grant system on the whole to be well-designed, with improvements desirable in the distribution of RSG.[8] A further report by the Institute developed four alternative equalisation models based on estimated needs and resources, with illustrations showing substantial redistribution of RSG in many cases.[9] The position at the time of writing is as set out by the Minister for the Environment in Dáil Eireann on 27 October 1994:

> I have explained to the House on a number of occasions that I do not consider that it would be practicable or appropriate to attempt a redistribution of the rate support grant on a basis such as that recommended by the Institute for Fiscal Studies some years ago.
>
> The present system of rate support grant allocations has evolved over a period of some sixteen years. Adjustments to the system made over the years have generally been financially neutral for the local authorities. Where increased overall allocations have been made available in the Estimates for a particular year, the additional funds have generally been allocated on a pro-rata basis among the local authorities.
>
> Proposals for a new distribution system must take realistic account of the present allocations so as to ensure that no area suffers unnecessarily through disruption of important services. Any new basis of allocation must also take account of the particular difficulties experienced by some local authorities. Where imbalances may exist under existing arrangements, they did not come about overnight and it would be imprudent to try to solve them otherwise than on a phased basis, possibly over a number of years.
>
> I will be taking account of factors such as the foregoing in settling the allocations for 1995 which I hope to be able to notify to local authorities shortly.[10]

It may reasonably be concluded that, given its technical

complexity and the issues at stake, equalisation can never be solely a matter of abstract models. Compromise and adaptation to the context involved must also be taken into account.[11]

Incentives

Where central government provides non-matching specific grants for particular projects/services and does not require local fiscal effort, problems could arise concerning the implications of such grants for the incentives facing local authorities.

In the case of national projects/services being financed in full by central government, the local authority (acting as agent of central government) has no direct financial incentive at evaluation or implementation stage to exercise the most rigorous appraisal and cost control systems. There is a risk that costs will be incurred that might otherwise be avoided if the ultimate funding body were directly in charge of the project/service. While central government would have the lead role in relation to project/service evaluation taking an overview of national requirements, it is the local authority which is best placed at implementation stage to ensure that costs are kept to the minimum consistent with achievement of the objectives of the project/service. This point highlights the need for effective systems to monitor and contain the cost of projects/services of this type.

In cases where non-matching specific grants are provided for projects/services the benefits from which accrue, at least in part, to the local area, further problems could arise. In these circumstances, not only does the local authority have no direct financial incentive to appraise or prioritise projects/services or to assiduously oversee them at implementation stage. There may also be a risk of the authority seeking to have as many projects as possible approved or services provided for its area without the level of appraisal which would occur if costs as well as benefits were being fully weighed against each other. While central government retains the power to determine which projects are to proceed or services to be provided, projects/services could be promoted at local level without sufficient regard to factors other than local benefits. This point highlights the importance of appropriate design of grant schemes.

Assigned Revenues

In some countries local authorities are allocated a pre-determined share of certain national taxes. The total level of these taxes and the proportion allocated locally are determined by central government. Allocation of particular revenues to local authorities is one means of determining the level of central government grants to local government and, depending on the operational arrangements, it can introduce an element of certainty to local government finance. It may also be argued, however, that the amount of central government grants to local authorities should be determined in the light of the overall need for local authority services, the resources of local authorities and the general national policy in relation to the aggregate level of tax and public expenditure, rather than by factors such as the amount raised in particular national taxes. The latter approach could, on this view, inhibit central government from making changes in the structure of national taxation which would be desirable but for their impact on local authorities.

Conclusion

Central government grants may be used to finance local government in whole or in part, to meet the cost of national services or to promote equalisation. The principal distinction between such grants is whether they are general or specific. A central government general grant is used in Ireland to supplement other sources of income; specific grants are availed of to assist in the provision of particular services; and there is heavy reliance on specific non-matching grants. Issues to be considered include the extent to which grants adequately reflect varying needs and resources across local authorities, the implications of specific non-matching grants for the incentives they face and the desirability or otherwise of a system of assigned revenues.

NOTES TO CHAPTER 7

1. This option is summarised in NESC, *The Financing of Local Authorities*, Dublin: NESC (1985), pp. 6, 35, 44 and 84-87

2. This typology is taken from L. Oulasvirta, 'Municipal Public Finance in the Nordic Countries', *Local Government Studies*, Winter 1993, p. 109

3. *Social Housing – The Way Ahead*, Dublin: Department of the Environment (1995), pp. 13-14; Department of the Environment Press Release, 8 August 1995

4. The word 'broadly' is used because, in addition to the deductions from RSG to take account of the elimination of various expenditure requirements (see chapter 2), other adjustments took place – additional funding was given to certain local authorities in 1994 and 1995 as part of RSG to meet accumulated deficits and to deal with other structural problems (*Official Report of Dail Debates*, 11 October 1994, Question No. 241 and 23 January 1996, Question No 273)

5. Arguments along these lines are advanced in NESC, *op. cit.*, pp. 86-8

6. *Report of Advisory Expert Committee on Local Government Reorganisation and Reform*, Dublin: Stationery Office (1991), p. (iii)

7. Ibid., p. 39

8. Institute for Fiscal Studies, 'Report on the Role of Central Grants in Local Finance in the Republic of Ireland', printed as supplement to *Report of Advisory Expert Committee, op.cit.*, p. 6

9. Institute for Fiscal Studies, *Rate Support Grant Distribution in Ireland*, Dublin: Stationery Office (1992)

10. *Official Report of Dail Debates*, 27 October 1994, Questions Nos. 3 and 19

11. This section draws generally on P. Blair, 'Financial Equalisation Between Local and Regional Authorities in European Countries', *Local Government Studies*, Winter 1993, pp. 7-27

8
Charges for Services

Introduction

This chapter considers the principles which should apply in charging for the services provided by local authorities, as well as some arguments which may be taken into account in determining if charging is appropriate. It also looks at the scope for increasing local authority income from miscellaneous sources and from domestic service charges. Finally, the issue of outsourcing is discussed.

Principles of Charging

There are a number of principles regarding charges for services:

- the greater the public good element of the service, the less feasible it is administratively to charge the full economic, or indeed any, cost;
- the greater the merit good element of the service, the less appropriate it is to charge the full economic cost if public policy objectives are to be met;
- the charge may with benefit be linked to the cost of the service received and the volume of the service consumed;
- the costs of collection should be justifiable.

The extent to which a service is supplying a public rather than a private good is important in the context of charges. Most public services contain both elements e.g. public lighting undoubtedly benefits the households outside which it is provided, but the main benefit arises to the public at large who use the roads and footpaths that are lit. It is usually not feasible to levy direct user charges in respect of services benefiting the public at large.

Providing public services to recipients at less than the full economic cost can be an important means of redistributing income in society. While some might argue that it would be preferable to give people an adequate income and charge the full economic cost of public services, this is impracticable. It may also be undesirable in that it would reduce the consumption of merit goods. For services whose primary function is a redistributive one, any attempt to charge the full economic cost would defeat the objective. It has been argued that it is inappropriate for any major redistributive function to be financed, whether by charges or taxes, at the local as opposed to the national level; the main services with a primary redistributive aim (education, health and welfare) are arranged and financed at the national level.[1]

Apart from the considerations applying to public goods and merit goods, user charges may be justified for two reasons. First, they have a role in providing signals for efficient resource allocation. Charges on the basis of cost and usage provide people with an incentive to reduce demand. Secondly, the revenue raised helps to reduce the rate of growth in taxation. The advantages of using charges as a means of environmental management are discussed in chapter 6.

While at a theoretical level efficiency and equity can be served by linking charges to the cost of the service and to the volume of the service consumed, this must be balanced against the costs of assessment and collection, which must be justified in the light of the revenue raised, and against the need for waiver schemes to ensure that people who are unable to pay are not deprived of essential services.

Miscellaneous Local Authority Income

As we have seen in chapter 2, miscellaneous sources of income constitute about 36 per cent of current local authority income. While it would appear that there should be scope to utilise these sources for additional discretionary income, there are constraints on local authorities in endeavouring to do this:

• loan repayments by those purchasing or improving houses are the largest source of such income, but the level of income is fixed by reference to the cost of funds to local authorities, and such income goes to meet repayments by local authorities of their borrowings. Indeed, to the extent that difficulties are encountered in securing repayments from householders, this programme can create financial problems for local authorities who have their own repayment obligations to meet;

- rents paid by tenants of local authority houses are determined by local authorities themselves, having regard to guidelines provided by the Department of the Environment. The aggregate cost of management and maintenance of the local authority housing stock was £88 million in 1993 compared to a rental income of £52 million, current account tenant purchase payments (see below) of £21 million and miscellaneous related receipts of £6 million; these are aggregate figures and the position varied from one local authority to another.[2] The major constraint faced by individual local authorities in any endeavour to move to economic rents is the fact that most tenants rely wholly or mainly on social welfare payments as their source of income: at the end of 1993, 82 per cent of tenants were in that position, and at the end of 1994, rent arrears amounted to £13 million.[3] To the extent that rents are below an economic level, the cost must be borne elsewhere in local authority budgets;

- tenants can buy out their local authority houses under purchase schemes, the terms of which are determined at central government level. The price to be paid by tenant purchasers under the 1995 scheme is the market value, less discounts of 3 per cent for each year of tenancy (with a maximum of 30 per cent) and of a further £3000.[4] Under pre-1993 schemes, 40 per cent of the proceeds of sales could be used by local authorities for the benefit of their current accounts with the balance being credited to capital to help finance the local authority housing capital programme. Under the terms of schemes since 1993, all of the proceeds have to be used for housing capital purposes and so this source of current income, which in any event is fixed in amount, is diminishing over time as the payments involved under the pre-1993 schemes come progressively to an end;

- in the interests of equity, local domestic service charges are waived in cases of hardship and, as in the case of local authority rents, the cost must be met at local level. Waivers are granted at the discretion of individual local authorities but guidelines on the operation of such schemes have been given to local authorities by the Department of the Environment. The cost of waivers of domestic service charges in terms of income foregone amounted to £9.1 million in 1993;[5]

- commercial/industrial consumers of large quantities of water are charged for the supply on the basis of usage although smaller-scale users are not;

- the level of fees in respect of planning applications (and of any subsequent appeals to An Bord Pleanala) is determined by central government. The current fees are set out in the Local Government (Planning and Development) Regulations, 1994 made by the Minister for the Environment;

- local authorities (in the case of non-national roads) and the National Roads Authority (in the case of national roads) may, subject to the approval of the Minister for the Environment, charge tolls for use of existing or new public roads under the provisions of the Roads Act, 1993 (Part V). Such road pricing may be implemented to pay for capital or current costs, to reduce traffic and associated pollution, or generally to secure efficient use of an expensive resource by charging for its use. However, tolling on a wide scale faces the problem of public resistance, difficulties in restricting access to tolled roads and likely diversion of traffic to less suitable routes. In practice, tolling has only been considered in the context of proposals for major new roads and just two roads in Ireland – the East Link and West Link Bridges in Dublin, both of which involved private finance in their construction – are tolled at present;[6]

- many services are small-scale in nature and could not realistically be expected to make an appreciable contribution to local government finance.

Domestic Service Charges

Domestic service charges are one category of miscellaneous receipts. The Local Government (Financial Provisions) (No. 2) Act, 1983 widened considerably the powers of local authorities to charge for domestic services. Up until then there had been a variety of restrictions on what could be charged for and the amounts to be charged. Removal of these restrictions opened the way for the introduction of new or increased charges in many local authority areas; the principal service charged for is water supply, with charges in some cases also for sewerage facilities and domestic refuse collection.

A feature of the current system is the extensive but uneven use of charges. For example, Dublin and Limerick Corporations made no water charges in 1996 and Waterford County Council has a charge of £145. The nature and extent of charges are matters for each local authority to decide – in particular the elected members, as the levying of such charges is a function reserved to them. Table 10 sets out the domestic service charges levied by each local authority in 1996.

The revenue raised from domestic service charges is significant, amounting to about £55 million in 1995. In that year, revenue from such charges amounted to nearly 5 per cent of total current income and they are generally viewed by local authorities as an important source of discretionary income.

From the outset these charges were controversial and they have remained so. The consultants for NESC reported in 1985: 'When domestic rates were abolished/transferred, income tax was increased to meet the revenue shortfall and thus to cover the cost of services previously financed from rates – such as water, at least in the urban areas. It was apparent from our discussions that many people consider that to levy water charges now, on top of the higher taxes, is to charge twice for the same service.'[7] As against this, it can be argued that the increased use of domestic service charges since 1983 is only one of many developments in the financing of public services in the past decade, developments which have included the stabilisation and later reduction of the overall burden of taxation as a proportion of national income.

Table 10: Domestic Service Charges 1996 (£)

COUNTY COUNCILS	WATER	REFUSE	SEWERAGE	TOTAL 1996
CARLOW	88	PRIVATISED	44	132
CAVAN	105	60	60	225
CLARE	120	60–70	NO CHARGE	180–190
CORK N	85	75p PER TAG	NO CHARGE	85
CORK V.B. S	63–75	45	NO CHARGE	108–120
CORK W	88	53	NO CHARGE	141
DONEGAL	130	PRIVATISED	NO CHARGE	130
D.LÀOIRE/R.DOWN	52–95	NO CHARGE	NO CHARGE	52–95
FINGAL	85	PRIVATISED	NO CHARGE	85
GALWAY	127	NO CHARGE	50	177
KERRY	115	76 DISC	50	165
KILDARE	80	65	NO CHARGE	145
KILKENNY	100	50p PER TAG	NO CHARGE	100
LAOIS	130	NO CHARGE	NO CHARGE	130
LEITRIM	115	PRIVATISED	NO CHARGE	115
LIMERICK V.B.	88–100	65p PER TAG	NO CHARGE	88–100
LONGFORD	115	PRIVATISED	30	145
LOUTH	128	PRIVATISED	NO CHARGE	128
MAYO	105	70	50	225
MEATH	123	PRIVATISED	NO CHARGE	123
MONAGHAN	86	50	NO CHARGE	136
OFFALY	95	PRIVATISED	20	115

Table 10: (contd).

ROSCOMMON	120	PRIVATISED	30	150
SLIGO	110	PRIVATISED	50	160
STH DUBLIN	70	NO CHARGE	NO CHARGE	70
TIPPERARY N.R.	120	NO CHARGE	50	170
TIPPERARY S.R.	120	80	NO CHARGE	200
WATERFORD	145	2 PER TAG	NO CHARGE	145
WESTMEATH	117	39	32	188
WEXFORD	125	55–70	NO CHARGE	180–195
WICKLOW	60	58	61	179

COUNTY BOROUGH CORPORATIONS

CORK V.B.	51–125.50	46	NO CHARGE	97–171.50
DUBLIN	NO CHARGE	NO CHARGE	NO CHARGE	NO CHARGE
GALWAY	66	NO CHARGE	NO CHARGE	66
LIMERICK	NO CHARGE	NO CHARGE	NO CHARGE	NO CHARGE
WATERFORD V.B.	50–150	NO CHARGE	NO CHARGE	50–150

BOROUGH CORPORATIONS

CLONMEL	85	60	NO CHARGE	145
DROGHEDA	75	NO CHARGE	NO CHARGE	75
KILKENNY	93	10	28	103
SLIGO	28	29	NO CHARGE	85
WEXFORD	51	37		88

Table 10: (contd).

URBAN DISTRICT COUNCILS		WATER	REFUSE	SEWERAGE	TOTAL 1996
ARKLOW	V.B	43.33-50	43.34-50	43.33-50	130-150
ATHLONE		108	28	28	164
ATHY		63-73	57	NO CHARGE	120-130
BALLINA		95	45	NO CHARGE	140
BALLINASLOE		90	PRIVATISED	18	108
BIRR		85	NO CHARGE	15	100
BRAY	V.B	101-134	NO CHARGE	NO CHARGE	101-134
BUNCRANA		120	NO CHARGE	NO CHARGE	120
BUNDORAN		110	NO CHARGE	NO CHARGE	110
CARLOW		75	39	33	147
CARRICKMACROSS		75	PRIVATISED	NO CHARGE	75
CARRICK-ON-SUIR		65	55	10	130
CASHEL		60	65	15	140
CASTLEBAR		100	50	NO CHARGE	150
CASTLEBLAYNEY		URBAN 75	NO CHARGE	NO CHARGE	75
		RURAL 85	NO CHARGE	NO CHARGE	85
CAVAN		105	55	30	190
CLONAKILTY		88	48	NO CHARGE	136
CLONES		URBAN 95	30	NO CHARGE	125
		RURAL 115	30	NO CHARGE	145
COBH		57	45	NO CHARGE	102
DUNDALK		105	35	NO CHARGE	140
DUNGARVAN		60	NO CHARGE	NO CHARGE	60
ENNIS		110	48	NO CHARGE	158

Table 10: (contd).

ENNISCORTHY	108	33p PER TAG	NO CHARGE	108
FERMOY	80	60p-75p	NO CHARGE	80
KELLS	120	NO CHARGE	NO CHARGE	120
KILLARNEY V.B.	45-108	45-60	21-25	111-193
KILRUSH	110	NO CHARGE	NO CHARGE	110
KINSALE	55	40	NO CHARGE	95
LETTERKENNY	120	PRIVATISED	NO CHARGE	120
LISTOWEL	67	62 P.A. 14.25 PER QTR	36	165
LONGFORD	81	25	56	162
MACROOM	54	54	NO CHARGE	108
MALLOW	36.50	36.50	NO CHARGE	73
MIDLETON	52	40	NO CHARGE	92
MONAGHAN V.B.	85	50	NO CHARGE	135
NAAS	76	50	NO CHARGE	126
NAVAN	81	NO CHARGE	NO CHARGE	81
NENAGH	34	10	36	80
NEW ROSS	65	NO CHARGE	NO CHARGE	65
SKIBBEREEN	82	50	NO CHARGE	132
TEMPLEMORE	60	NO CHARGE	50	110
THURLES V.B.	65-75	NO CHARGE	15	80-90
TIPPERARY	50	55	25	130
TRALEE V.B.	72-92	40	40	152-172
TRIM	107	PRIVATISED	NO CHARGE	107
TULLAMORE	85	NO CHARGE	20	105
WESTPORT	74	39	NO CHARGE	113
WICKLOW	55	54	43	152
YOUGAL	63	35	NO CHARGE	98

V.B.:VALUATION BASED.   *Source: Official Report of Dail Debates*, 23 January 1996, Question No. 297

In technical terms, double taxation has a precise meaning in taxation literature which defines it as the phenomenon of income flow being subjected to more than one charge to tax under the *same* domestic tax system. An example of this is the taxation of distributed company profits under a classical system of corporation tax, where dividends are taxed fully in the hands of the recipient and no relief is given for tax borne on the same income flow at the company level. Double taxation is not deemed to occur where the charge does not arise under the same tax system. For example, it is not considered to occur when a taxpayer is asked to pay VAT on expenditure out of income which has been fully charged to income tax. The view that domestic service charges are a form of double taxation is not, therefore, based on the strict taxation definition of the concept.

This view did however persist and influenced central government policy: from 1995 amounts paid in domestic service charges can be set off as an allowance against income tax due (at the standard rate up to a maximum allowance of £150). This allowance will commence in the tax year 1996-97 for charges paid in 1995. Legislation has also been introduced to circumscribe the operation of the power of local authorities to disconnect consumers for non-payment of domestic water charges.[8] These actions were taken in the context of a commitment in a programme for government to 'a professional study to see how a fair, equitable and reasonable system of funding can be introduced with a view to publishing a White Paper on the subject and seeking to develop the maximum degree of consensus on the issue'.[9]

Most domestic service charges are levied on a basis other than the level of usage of the service. While flat-rate charges have the advantage of administrative simplicity, they do not generally act to promote efficient use of the service. According to Table 10, 'tag-on-the-bag' or other volume-related systems are used in six local authority areas to charge for domestic refuse collection; however, twenty-three local authorities do not charge for this service and forty-seven levy fixed charges. Charges where levied do not generally meet internal, let alone external, costs.[10] It has been suggested that consideration should be given to metering of domestic water supplies, and charging on that basis, but local authorities have not chosen to follow that route because of concern about the costs involved.[11]

Outsourcing

An alternative means of providing public services is to divorce overall control of the service from its actual production – the so-called 'purchaser/provider split'. This may provide a means of clearly identifying the costs of services for which it is desired to charge. In this case, the local authority may still determine the level of service provided but is free to purchase it from some outside agency. Outsourcing may be appropriate where the flow of work is uneven throughout the year and where the need for staff to cope with peak volumes may lead to excess capacity during valley periods. It may also be appropriate in areas of work which are changing rapidly such as technology.

Outsourcing enables the provider of a service to be subject to the market disciplines of competition at appropriate intervals when the contract for the provision of the service comes up for renewal. A further point is that it frees management of the local authority from the responsibility of day-to-day management of individual services which may not be their primary area of expertise. However, it is important to specify clearly the standards of service that must be provided and to have appropriate means of evaluating that these standards are met. The extent to which efficiency gains might be achieved through a deterioration in conditions of employment is also relevant from the point of view of public policy.

Local authorities in Ireland already make extensive use of external sources of service provision:

- financial pressures on local authorities have led to a reduction in the number of local authority direct labour workers, who now concentrate primarily on maintenance-type work;

- major capital projects (roads, housing, water/sewerage) are subject to competitive tendering, often on an EU-wide basis;
- considerable use is made of private sector consulting engineers in the planning, design and implementation of such projects, and of private sector legal services;
- the domestic refuse collection service has been contracted out, franchised or privatised in many areas, in the latter case the local authority withdrawing from the service and allowing private contractors to take over and charge for the service;
- as mentioned above, private finance has been used to meet the capital cost of the East Link and West Link Bridges in Dublin and is being remunerated by means of tolls;
- private group water schemes, with Exchequer assistance, continue to make a significant contribution to meeting water supply needs in rural areas;
- local authority houses are sold to tenants under tenant purchase schemes;
- there is increased support for, and reliance on, the voluntary housing sector to meet social housing needs;
- partnerships with the private sector are increasingly common in the context of urban renewal and local development initiatives, and the provision of local amenities.

When considering the scope for further use of outsourcing, account must be taken of the limited range of Irish local government services, the extent of outsourcing already in place, the need for local authorities to respond to emergency situations and the generally non-ideological approach to such issues which has been followed to date in this country. It has been suggested, however, that greater use will need to be made of private finance to meet prospective infrastructural needs in the roads, water, sewerage and waste disposal areas.[12]

Conclusion

The extent to which a good is a public good or a merit good, and the costs of assessment and collection, are factors which influence the decision whether to charge for a service. Charges have, however, potential to improve the allocation of resources in particular cases. The scope for increased local authority income from miscellaneous receipts is in practice limited.

Domestic service charges provide a source of discretionary income for local authorities but they have been the subject of public controversy. The nature and extent of such charges vary between local authorities but flat-rate charges for water supply are most common. Outsourcing is an alterative means by which services may be provided but local authorities in Ireland already make extensive use of external sources of service provision.

NOTES TO CHAPTER 8

1. NESC, *The Financing of Local Authorities*, Dublin : NESC (1985), pp. 45-6

2. Department of the Environment, *Annual Housing Statistics Bulletin 1994*, Dublin: Stationery Office (1995), p. 45

3. *Official Report of Dail Debates*, 2 March 1995, Question No. 71

4. *Social Housing – The Way Ahead*, Dublin: Department of the Environment (1995), p.31

5. *Official Report of Dail Debates*, 16 May 1995, Question No. 139

6. Government policy in relation to tolling of national roads is set out in *Ireland -National Development Plan 1994-1999*, Dublin: Stationery Office (1993), p. 100. See also *Official Report of Dail Debates*, 7 November 1995, Question No. 4

7. NESC, *op. cit.*, p. 29

8. Finance Act, 1995 (section 7), and the Local Government (Delimitation of Water Supply Disconnection Powers) Act, 1995

9. *Policy Agreement, A Government of Renewal*, Dublin: (1995), pp. 50-1

10. In the remaining 14 local authority areas, the collection is fully privatised. See also A. Barrett and J. Lawlor, *The Economics of Solid Waste Management in Ireland*, ESRI Policy Research Series, Paper No. 28, November 1995

11. NESC, *op. cit.*, p. 48. For a relevent recent analysis *see* 'Generale Des Eaux and M.C. O'Sullivan and Co. Ltd.', *Greater Dublin Water Supply Strategy*, Dublin, Department of the Environment (1996), Chapter 14

12. C. Power,' Public Funding Worries', *Management*, September 1995

9
Conclusion

The Problem of Local Government Finance
One of the problems with local government finance is lack of agreement on the nature of the problem. It is possible to discern at least four distinct, though related, views on what constitutes the issue to be addressed.

Lack of Income
On this view, the problem with local government finance is that local authorities have insufficient income. This gives rise in particular to heavy reliance on expensive overdraft or other short-term borrowing to finance structural deficits on current accounts.[1] One solution often canvassed is increased central government funding of local authorities.

Evidence for this view includes the limited rate increases (below inflation) allowed by central government in 1978-82[2]; a shortfall in 1982 in the level of the domestic rate grant compared to the amount due based on the level of rate increase permitted[3]; the loss of £20 million to local authorities as a result of the end of agricultural rates in 1982; the difference between RSG and rates income foregone by local authorities in subsequent years; and difficulties in levying and collecting revenue from water and other domestic service charges.

Excessive Expenditure Commitments
A second view of the problem also focuses on the financial condition of local authorities, but would see the problem as lying mainly in the growth of the role of local authorities in recent decades in services such as environmental protection, operation

and maintenance of new water supply and sewerage facilities, implementation of building regulations, and promotion of, and participation in, urban and village renewal initiatives. The additional demands thereby placed on local authorities, coupled with rising pay costs determined at central government level (without the consequent increases in grants usually made available in these circumstances to non-commercial semi-state bodies), are seen as having played a significant role in the deteriorating financial position of local authorities.

Limited Local Discretion

It is a common, though not universal, view that one essential feature of systems of local government is the power to set the levels of, and to collect, local taxation to finance the provision of services for the benefit of the local community. On this view, the problem with Irish local government finance stems from the narrowing of the local taxation base by the abolition of domestic rates in 1978 and the end of rates on land in 1982, and their non-replacement by alternative forms of local taxation. Even allowing for the continuation of commercial/industrial rates, proponents of this view argue that one of the principal pillars of democratic local self-government is absent, or has been significantly diminished.

Insufficient Accountability

This relates to what is seen as a lack of accountability, on the part of those in local authorities responsible for expenditure decisions, to those national taxpayers and local commercial/industrial ratepayers who meet most of the cost of providing local services. National taxation is set by central government and falls unevenly across the various local authority areas in ways unrelated to the level of local services; commercial/industrial rates are set locally but are not for the most part borne directly by those who vote in local elections. In these ways, the financing of local authorities is seen as defective in terms of the mechanisms in place to ensure that taxpayers can call to account those responsible for local expenditure and taxation decisions.

Constraints on Solutions

Any solution to the problem of local government finance depends, of course, on how the problem is defined. There are constraints surrounding many of the solutions suggested over the years.

If the problem is seen as one of limited resources, the remedy of increased central government funding of local authorities might seem to be a relatively painless approach. The main difficulty here is the determination of central government to maintain tight control of the public finances as a whole, and the likelihood that it will not be able to divert large-scale additional resources to the local authority or indeed to any other sector.

Alternatively, efforts to address financial difficulties through action on the expenditure side of the accounts are not likely to produce quick and painless results. While the need to seek greater efficiency in the use of resources would always be a concern of local authority management, it may not be realistic to expect significant benefits in the short-term. If this is so, then the only option which remains on the expenditure side in terms of short-term action is retrenchment in the actual level of services.

The most widely-proffered solution is the introduction of a new property tax levied and collected by local authorities. This would, it is suggested by its proponents, strengthen local democracy and, by impacting on local electors, significantly improve accountability. The extra revenue generated would allow scaling-back of the level of central government support for local authorities, enabling other taxes to be reduced. However, depending on the nature of the property tax system proposed, this solution would benefit some while increasing the tax burden of others.

Furthermore, since 1987 central government has followed a consensual approach to economic and social policy as embodied in the Programme for National Recovery, the Programme for Economic and Social Progress, and the Programme for Competitiveness and Work. Unfettered discretion for local authorities to set significantly increased levels of local taxation might be seen by some as upsetting the efforts by such programmes to set rates of pay and taxation in conjunction with the social partners, and to reach agreement at that level on developments in public services. It could also be argued that such an approach would militate against central government control of overall public expenditure and taxation as part of management of the macro-economy, possibly prejudicing objectives set for these variables at national level. However, the relative importance of this in a very small and open economy like Ireland, with a small–scale local government system, could be over-stated. Finally, it is evident from Table 8 that local income, rather than local property, taxes are the mainstay of local government in those countries with which Ireland is often compared.

The Future

The future is difficult, often impossible, to predict. There is little point in attempting to identify in precise terms what is going to happen to local government finance in the years ahead, but it is profitable to try to sketch out broad trends which might affect the issues addressed in this text.

It seems clear from the adverse experience of the 1980s, numerous Government policy statements in the years since then and prospective developments at EU level in the context of proposed economic and monetary union, that a disciplined approach to management of the public finances and downward pressure on the overall level of taxation will continue. As suggested above, central government is unlikely to divert large-scale additional resources to the local authority or any other sector. This applies in terms of the prospect of increased direct central government funding. It also applies, however, in the event of any decision to increase significantly the level of local taxation; it is now commonly accepted that such a decision would be accompanied by a comparable scaling-back of central government funding of local authorities so as to allow reductions elsewhere in the taxation system.[4]

The EU is likely to continue to have a major influence on public policy in Ireland. Although EU developments are especially difficult to predict, it is reasonable to assume that there will be some further widening and deepening of the Union. In particular, the accession in 1995 of Austria, Finland and Sweden is likely to be followed at some stage by the entry of central and eastern European states. These states, given their stage of economic development, will place considerable additional demands on EU structural/cohesion resources and will inevitably provide competition in this regard for the traditional four 'cohesion' countries. Things may also become more difficult for Ireland on this front due to the progress being made in bringing living standards up to the EU average: Ireland's GNP per capita was 71 per cent of the EU average in 1994[5] and the ESRI, in their study of medium-term economic prospects, use the working assumption that structural assistance to Ireland will fall to 50 per cent of present levels from the year 2000.[6]

There may also be pressures to change the procedures for the management of EU funds in Ireland. If, at some stage in the future, Ireland no longer qualifies as a single region for structural funding, the question may arise as to whether certain parts of the country can continue to benefit from such funding due to disparities of income within Ireland. If only particular areas qualify, this will raise in a new way the issue of the role of central government in the disbursement of EU funds and whether bodies in the qualifying areas, including local authorities, are to be given greater direct access to the funds without mediation by central government.

There will be continued public demand for more and better public services – a demand which is unlikely to be satiated by the prospective rise in private income and consumption in the coming years. This insistence on more will not be accompanied by a willingness to pay more: on the contrary, public resistance can be expected to any new or additional taxes. These pressures will be accentuated by technological advances which will mean that more can actually done in terms of service provision – at a price – than previously thought possible. Local authorities, as the frontline providers of many public services, will not be immune from these trends.

These paragraphs appear to offer little solace to those

concerned with local government finance: limited prospects for a large-scale injection of resources from central government, uncertainty surrounding the EU funds which underwrite a number of the major local authority expenditure programmes, public demand for improved services without a willingness to accept the implications this may have for taxation. None of these trends is, however, new and together they amount to no more than a challenge on a scale faced by most public and private sector organisations today. The question which remains is whether local government will be able to meet that challenge; the answer lies largely, though not exclusively, in the hands of local government itself and of those who serve the public at local level.

NOTES TO CHAPTER 9

1. Overdraft interest cost local authorities £3.4 million in 1993 and £1.7 million in 1994 (*Official Report of Dail Debates,* 27 October 1994, Question No. 52 and 28 November 1995, Question No. 116)
2. R. B. Haslam and N. Collins, 'Local Government Finance in the Republic of Ireland – The Aftermath of Rates Abolition', in R. Paddison and S. Bailey (eds.), *Local Government Finance: International Perspectives,* London: Routledge (1988), p. 222
3. *Ibid.*, pp. 222-3
4. For example, see the Fourth Report of the Commission on Taxation*, Special Taxation*, Dublin: Stationery Office (1985), paragraph 5.44 and NESC, *The Financing of Local Authorities*, Dublin: NESC (1985), p. 9
5. Central Bank, *Annual Report 1994*, p. 8
6. *ESRI, Medium-Term Review 1994-2000*, Dublin: ESRI (1994), p. 36

INDEX